HOLT SCIENCE & TECHNOLOGY

Electricity and Magnetism

HOLT, RINEHART AND WINSTON

A Harcourt Classroom Education Company

Austin · New York · Orlando · Atlanta · San Francisco · Boston · Dallas · Toronto · London

Staff Credits

Editorial

Robert W. Todd, Executive Editor

Anne Earvolino, Senior Editor

Michael Mazza, Ken Shepardson, Kelly Rizk, Bill Burnside, Editors

ANCILLARIES

Jennifer Childers, Senior Editor

Chris Colby, Molly Frohlich, Shari Husain, Kristen McCardel, Sabelyn Pussman, Erin Roberson

COPYEDITING

Dawn Spinozza, Copyediting Supervisor

EDITORIAL SUPPORT STAFF

Jeanne Graham, Mary Helbling, Tanu'e White, Doug Rutley

EDITORIAL PERMISSIONS

Cathy Paré, Permissions Manager

Jan Harrington, Permissions Editor

Art, Design, and Photo

BOOK DESIGN

Richard Metzger, Design Director

Marc Cooper, Senior Designer

Ron Bowdoin, Designer

Alicia Sullivan, Designer (ATE),

Cristina Bowerman, Design Associate (ATE)

Eric Rupprath, Designer (Ancillaries)

Holly Whittaker, Traffic Coordinator

IMAGE ACQUISITIONS

Joe London, Director

Elaine Tate, Art Buyer Supervisor

Tim Taylor, Photo Research Supervisor

Stephanie Morris, Assistant Photo Researcher

PHOTO STUDIO

Sam Dudgeon, Senior Staff Photographer

Victoria Smith, Photo Specialist

Lauren Eischen, Photo Coordinator

DESIGN NEW MEDIA

Susan Michael, Design Director

Production

Mimi Stockdell, Senior Production Manager

Beth Sample, Senior Production Coordinator

Suzanne Brooks, Sara Carroll-Downs

Media Production

Kim A. Scott, Senior Production Manager

Adriana Bardin-Prestwood, Senior Production Coordinator

New Media

Armin Gutzmer, Director

Jim Bruno, Senior Project Manager

Lydia Doty, Senior Project Manager

Jessica Bega, Project Manager

Cathy Kuhles, Nina Degollado, Technical Assistants

Design Implementation and Production

The Quarasan Group, Inc.

Acknowledgments

Chapter Writers

Christie Borgford, Ph.D.
Professor of Chemistry
University of Alabama
Birmingham, Alabama

Andrew Champagne
Former Physics Teacher
Ashland High School
Ashland, Massachusetts

Mapi Cuevas, Ph.D.
Professor of Chemistry
Santa Fe Community College
Gainesville, Florida

Leila Dumas
Former Physics Teacher
LBJ Science Academy
Austin, Texas

William G. Lamb, Ph.D.
Science Teacher and Dept. Chair
Oregon Episcopal School
Portland, Oregon

Sally Ann Vonderbrink, Ph.D.
Chemistry Teacher
St. Xavier High School
Cincinnati, Ohio

Lab Writers

Phillip G. Bunce
Former Physics Teacher
Bowie High School
Austin, Texas

Kenneth E. Creese
Science Teacher
White Mountain Junior High School
Rock Springs, Wyoming

William G. Lamb, Ph.D.
Science Teacher and Dept. Chair
Oregon Episcopal School
Portland, Oregon

Alyson Mike
Science Teacher
East Valley Middle School
East Helena, Montana

Joseph W. Price
Science Teacher and Dept. Chair
H. M. Browne Junior High School
Washington, D.C.

Denice Lee Sandefur
Science Teacher and Dept. Chair
Nucla High School
Nucla, Colorado

John Spadafino
Mathematics and Physics Teacher
Hackensack High School
Hackensack, New Jersey

Walter Woolbaugh
Science Teacher
Manhattan Junior High School
Manhattan, Montana

Academic Reviewers

Paul R. Berman, Ph.D.
Professor of Physics
University of Michigan
Ann Arbor, Michigan

Russell M. Brengelman, Ph.D.
Professor of Physics
Morehead State University
Morehead, Kentucky

John A. Brockhaus, Ph.D.
Director, Mapping, Charting and Geodesy Program
Department of Geography and Environmental Engineering
United States Military Academy
West Point, New York

Walter Bron, Ph.D.
Professor of Physics
University of California
Irvine, California

Andrew J. Davis, Ph.D.
Manager, ACE Science Center
Department of Physics
California Institute of Technology
Pasadena, California

Peter E. Demmin, Ed.D.
Former Science Teacher and Department Chair
Amherst Central High School
Amherst, New York

Roger Falcone, Ph.D.
Professor of Physics and Department Chair
University of California
Berkeley, California

Cassandra A. Fraser, Ph.D.
Assistant Professor of Chemistry
University of Virginia
Charlottesville, Virginia

L. John Gagliardi, Ph.D.
Associate Professor of Physics and Department Chair
Rutgers University
Camden, New Jersey

Gabriele F. Giuliani, Ph.D.
Professor of Physics
Purdue University
West Lafayette, Indiana

Roy W. Hann, Jr., Ph.D.
Professor of Civil Engineering
Texas A&M University
College Station, Texas

John L. Hubisz, Ph.D.
Professor of Physics
North Carolina State University
Raleigh, North Carolina

Samuel P. Kounaves, Ph.D.
Professor of Chemistry
Tufts University
Medford, Massachusetts

Karol Lang, Ph.D.
Associate Professor of Physics
The University of Texas
Austin, Texas

Gloria Langer, Ph.D.
Professor of Physics
University of Colorado
Boulder, Colorado

Phillip LaRoe
Professor
Helena College of Technology
Helena, Montana

Joseph A. McClure, Ph.D.
Associate Professor of Physics
Georgetown University
Washington, D.C.

LaMoine L. Motz, Ph.D.
Coordinator of Science Education
Department of Learning Services
Oakland County Schools
Waterford, Michigan

R. Thomas Myers, Ph.D.
Professor of Chemistry, Emeritus
Kent State University
Kent, Ohio

Hillary Clement Olson, Ph.D.
Research Associate
Institute for Geophysics
The University of Texas
Austin, Texas

David P. Richardson, Ph.D.
Professor of Chemistry
Thompson Chemical Laboratory
Williams College
Williamstown, Massachusetts

John Rigden, Ph.D.
Director of Special Projects
American Institute of Physics
Colchester, Vermont

Peter Sheridan, Ph.D.
Professor of Chemistry
Colgate University
Hamilton, New York

Vederaman Sriraman, Ph.D.
Associate Professor of Technology
Southwest Texas State University
San Marcos, Texas

Jack B. Swift, Ph.D.
Professor of Physics
The University of Texas
Austin, Texas

Atiq Syed, Ph.D.
Master Instructor of Mathematics and Science
Texas State Technical College
Harlingen, Texas

Leonard Taylor, Ph.D.
Professor Emeritus
Department of Electrical Engineering
University of Maryland
College Park, Maryland

Virginia L. Trimble, Ph.D.
Professor of Physics and Astronomy
University of California
Irvine, California

Acknowledgments (cont.)

Martin VanDyke, Ph.D.
Professor of Chemistry, Emeritus
Front Range Community
    College
Westminster, Colorado

Gabriela Waschewsky,
    Ph.D.
Science and Math Teacher
Emery High School
Emeryville, California

Safety Reviewer

Jack A. Gerlovich, Ph.D.
Associate Professor
School of Education
Drake University
Des Moines, Iowa

Teacher Reviewers

Barry L. Bishop
Science Teacher and Dept. Chair
San Rafael Junior High School
Ferron, Utah

Paul Boyle
Science Teacher
Perry Heights Middle School
Evansville, Indiana

Kenneth Creese
Science Teacher
White Mountain Junior High
    School
Rock Springs, Wyoming

Vicky Farland
Science Teacher and Dept. Chair
Centennial Middle School
Yuma, Arizona

Rebecca Ferguson
Science Teacher
North Ridge Middle School
North Richland Hills, Texas

Laura Fleet
Science Teacher
Alice B. Landrum Middle
    School
Ponte Vedra Beach, Florida

Jennifer Ford
Science Teacher and Dept. Chair
North Ridge Middle School
North Richland Hills, Texas

Susan Gorman
Science Teacher
North Ridge Middle School
North Richland Hills, Texas

C. John Graves
Science Teacher
Monforton Middle School
Bozeman, Montana

Dennis Hanson
Science Teacher and Dept. Chair
Big Bear Middle School
Big Bear Lake, California

David A. Harris
Science Teacher and Dept. Chair
The Thacher School
Ojai, California

Norman E. Holcomb
Science Teacher
Marion Local Schools
Maria Stein, Ohio

Kenneth J. Horn
Science Teacher and Dept. Chair
Fallston Middle School
Fallston, Maryland

Tracy Jahn
Science Teacher
Berkshire Junior-Senior High
    School
Canaan, New York

Kerry A. Johnson
Science Teacher
Isbell Middle School
Santa Paula, California

Drew E. Kirian
Science Teacher
Solon Middle School
Solon, Ohio

Harriet Knops
Science Teacher and Dept. Chair
Rolling Hills Middle School
El Dorado, California

Scott Mandel, Ph.D.
Director and Educational
    Consultant
Teachers Helping Teachers
Los Angeles, California

Thomas Manerchia
Former Science Teacher
Archmere Academy
Claymont, Delaware

Edith McAlanis
Science Teacher and Dept. Chair
Socorro Middle School
El Paso, Texas

Kevin McCurdy, Ph.D.
Science Teacher
Elmwood Junior High School
Rogers, Arkansas

Alyson Mike
Science Teacher
East Valley Middle School
East Helena, Montana

Donna Norwood
Science Teacher and Dept. Chair
Monroe Middle School
Charlotte, North Carolina

Joseph W. Price
Science Teacher and Dept. Chair
H. M. Browne Junior High
    School
Washington, D.C.

Terry J. Rakes
Science Teacher
Elmwood Junior High School
Rogers, Arkansas

Beth Richards
Science Teacher
North Middle School
Crystal Lake, Illinois

Elizabeth J. Rustad
Science Teacher
Crane Middle School
Yuma, Arizona

Rodney A. Sandefur
Science Teacher
Naturita Middle School
Naturita, Colorado

Helen Schiller
Science Teacher
Northwood Middle School
Taylors, South Carolina

Bert J. Sherwood
Science Teacher
Socorro Middle School
El Paso, Texas

Patricia McFarlane Soto
Science Teacher and Dept. Chair
G. W. Carver Middle School
Miami, Florida

David M. Sparks
Science Teacher
Redwater Junior High School
Redwater, Texas

Larry Tackett
Science Teacher and Dept. Chair
Andrew Jackson Middle School
Cross Lanes, West Virginia

Elsie N. Waynes
Science Teacher and Dept. Chair
R. H. Terrell Junior High School
Washington, D.C.

Sharon L. Woolf
Science Teacher
Langston Hughes Middle
    School
Reston, Virginia

Alexis S. Wright
Middle School Science
    Coordinator
Rye Country Day School
Rye, New York

Lee Yassinski
Science Teacher
Sun Valley Middle School
Sun Valley, California

John Zambo
Science Teacher
Elizabeth Ustach Middle School
Modesto, California

Electricity and Magnetism

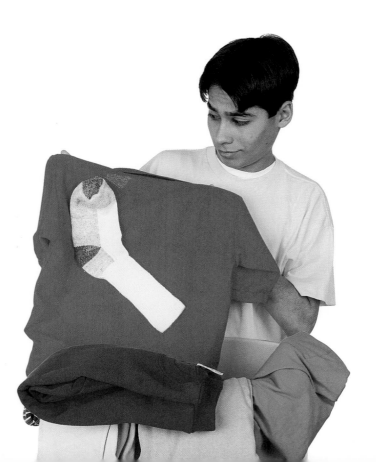

Contents   **v**

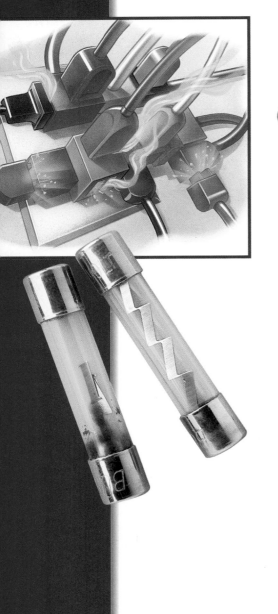

Skills Development

Process Skills

QuickLabs

Chapter Labs

Research and Critical Thinking Skills

Apply

Feature Articles

Science, Technology, and Society
Across the Sciences
Health Watch
Science Fiction

Connections

To the Student

This book was created to make your science experience interesting, exciting, and fun!

Go for It!

Science is a process of discovery, a trek into the unknown. The skills you develop using *Holt Science & Technology*— such as observing, experimenting, and explaining observations and ideas— are the skills you will need for the future. There is a universe of exploration and discovery awaiting those who accept the challenges of science.

Science & Technology

You see the interaction between science and technology every day. Science makes technology possible. On the other hand, some of the products of technology, such as computers, are used to make further scientific discoveries. In fact, much of the scientific work that is done today has become so technically complicated and expensive that no one person can do it entirely alone. But make no mistake, the creative ideas for even the most highly technical and expensive scientific work still come from individuals.

Activities and Labs

The activities and labs in this book will allow you to make some basic but important scientific discoveries on your own. You can even do some exploring on your own at home! Here's your chance to use your imagination and curiosity as you investigate your world.

Keep a ScienceLog

In this book, you will be asked to keep a type of journal called a ScienceLog to record your thoughts, observations, experiments, and conclusions. As you develop your ScienceLog, you will see your own ideas taking shape over time. You'll have a written record of how your ideas have changed as you learn about and explore interesting topics in science.

Know "What You'll Do"

The "What You'll Do" list at the beginning of each section is your built-in guide to what you need to learn in each chapter. When you can answer the questions in the Section Review and Chapter Review, you know you are ready for a test.

Check Out the Internet

You will see this  logo throughout the book. You'll be using *sci*LINKS as your gateway to the Internet. Once you log on to *sci*LINKS using your computer's Internet link, type in the *sci*LINKS address. When asked for the keyword code, type in the keyword for that topic. A wealth of resources is now at your disposal to help you learn more about that topic.

In addition to *sci*LINKS you can log on to some other great resources to go with your text. The addresses shown below will take you to the home page of each site.

This textbook contains the following on-line resources to help you make the most of your science experience.

Visit **go.hrw.com** for extra help and study aids matched to your textbook. Just type in the keyword HST HOME.

Visit **www.scilinks.org** to find resources specific to topics in your textbook. Keywords appear throughout your book to take you further.

 Smithsonian Institution® **Internet Connections**

Visit **www.si.edu/hrw** for specifically chosen on-line materials from one of our nation's premier science museums.

Visit **www.cnnfyi.com** for late-breaking news and current events stories selected just for you.

Contents   1

Introduction to Electricity

Pre-Reading Questions

1. What is static electricity, and how is it formed?
2. How is electrical energy produced?
3. What is a circuit, and what parts make up a circuit?

IT'S SHOCKING!

This eighth-grader is having fun learning firsthand about static electricity. She is touching a Van de Graaf generator, a device that produces positive electrical charges on the metal globe. These positive charges move through her body to the strands of hair on her head. Like charges repel each other, so each strand of her hair repels all the other hairs. In this chapter, you'll learn more about static electricity and how you use electrical energy in your everyday life.

CHARGE OVER MATTER

In this activity, you will make an electrically charged object and use it to pick up other objects.

Procedure

1. Cut **6–8 small squares of tissue paper.** Each square should be about 2 cm × 2 cm. Place the squares on your desk.

2. Hold a **plastic comb** close to the paper squares. Record what, if anything, happens.

3. Now rub the comb with a **piece of silk cloth** for about 30 seconds.

4. Hold the comb close to the tissue-paper squares, but don't touch them. Record your observations. If nothing happens, rub the comb for a little while longer and try again.

Analysis

5. When you rubbed the comb with the cloth, you gave the comb a negative electric charge. Why do you think this charge allowed you to pick up tissue-paper squares?

6. What other objects do you think you can use to pick up tissue-paper squares?

TRY at HOME

Terms to Learn

law of electric charges
electric force
conduction
induction

conductor
insulator
static electricity
electric discharge

What You'll Do

◆ State and give examples of the law of electric charges.
◆ Describe three ways an object can become charged.
◆ Compare conductors with insulators.
◆ Give examples of static electricity and electric discharge.

Electric Charge and Static Electricity

Have you ever reached out to open a door and received a shock from the knob? You may have been surprised, and your finger or hand probably felt tingly afterward. On dry days, you can easily produce shocks by shuffling your feet on a carpet and then lightly touching a metal object. These shocks are a result of a buildup of static electricity. But what is static electricity, and how is it formed? To answer these questions, you need to learn about charge.

Atoms and Charge

To investigate charge, you must know a little about the nature of matter. All matter is composed of very small particles called atoms. Atoms are made of even smaller particles called protons, neutrons, and electrons, as shown in **Figure 1.** One important difference between protons, neutrons, and electrons is that protons and electrons are charged particles and neutrons are not.

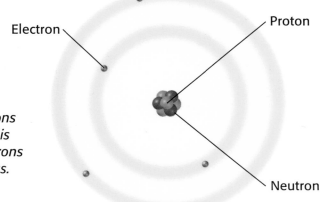

Figure 1 *Protons and neutrons make up the nucleus, which is the center of the atom. Electrons are found outside the nucleus.*

Electron

Proton

Neutron

Charges Can Exert Forces Charge is a physical property that is best understood by describing how charged objects interact with each other. A charged object exerts a force—a push or a pull—on other charged objects. There are two types of charge—positive and negative. The force between two charged objects varies depending on whether the objects have the same type of charge or opposite charges, as shown in **Figure 2.** The charged balls in Figure 2 illustrate the **law of electric charges,** which states that like charges repel and opposite charges attract.

Protons are positively charged, and electrons are negatively charged. Because protons and electrons are oppositely charged, protons and electrons are attracted to each other. If this attraction didn't exist, electrons would fly away from the nucleus of an atom.

Figure 2 *The law of electric charges states that like charges repel and opposite charges attract.*

Objects that have opposite charges are attracted to each other, and the force between the objects pulls them together.

Objects that have the same charge are repelled, and the force between the objects pushes them apart.

The Electric Force and the Electric Field The force between charged objects is an **electric force.** The strength of the electric force is determined by two factors. One factor is the size of the charges. The greater the charges are, the greater the electric force. The other factor that determines the strength of the electric force is the distance between the charges. The closer together the charges are, the greater the electric force.

The electric force exists because charged particles have electric fields around them. An *electric field* is a region around a charged particle that can exert a force on another charged particle. If a charged particle is in the electric field of another charged particle, the first particle is attracted or repelled by the electric force exerted on it.

Charge It!

Although an atom contains charged particles, the atom itself does not have a charge. Atoms contain an equal number of protons and electrons. Therefore, the positive and negative charges cancel each other out, and the atom has no overall charge. If the atoms of an object have no charge, how can the object become charged? Objects become charged because the atoms in the objects can gain or lose electrons. If the atoms of an object lose electrons, the object becomes positively charged. If the atoms gain electrons, the object becomes negatively charged. There are three common ways for an object to become charged—friction, conduction, and induction. When an object is charged by any method, no charges are created or destroyed. The charge on any object can be detected by a device called an electroscope.

Friction Rubbing two objects together can cause electrons to be "wiped" from one object and transferred to the other. If you rub a plastic ruler with a cloth, electrons are transferred from the cloth to the ruler. Because the ruler gains electrons, the ruler becomes negatively charged. Conversely, because the cloth loses electrons, the cloth becomes positively charged. **Figure 3** shows a fun example of objects becoming charged by friction.

Figure 3 *When you rub a balloon against your hair, electrons from your hair are transferred to the balloon.*

After the electrons are transferred, the balloon is negatively charged and your hair is positively charged.

Your hair and the balloon are attracted to each other because they are oppositely charged.

Conduction Charging by **conduction** occurs when electrons are transferred from one object to another by direct contact. For example, if you touch an uncharged piece of metal with a positively charged glass rod, electrons from the metal will move to the glass rod. Because the metal loses electrons, it becomes positively charged. **Figure 4** shows what happens when you touch a negatively charged object to an uncharged object.

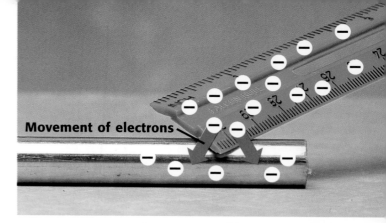

Figure 4 *Touching a negatively charged plastic ruler to an uncharged metal rod causes the electrons in the ruler to travel to the rod. The rod becomes negatively charged by conduction.*

Induction Charging by **induction** occurs when charges in an uncharged object are rearranged without direct contact with a charged object. For example, when a positively charged object is near a neutral object, the electrons in the neutral object are attracted to the positively charged object and move toward it. This movement produces a region of negative charge on the neutral object. **Figure 5** shows what happens when you hold a negatively charged balloon close to a neutral wall.

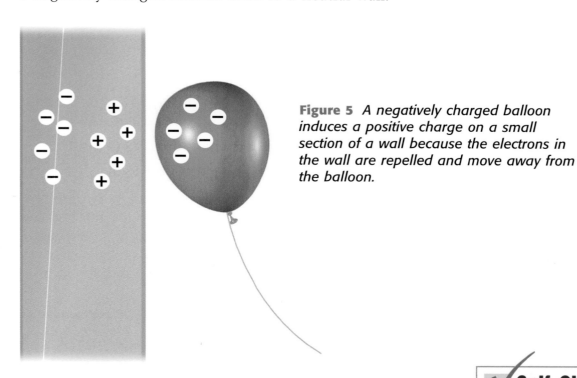

Figure 5 *A negatively charged balloon induces a positive charge on a small section of a wall because the electrons in the wall are repelled and move away from the balloon.*

Conservation of Charge When you charge objects by any method, no charges are created or destroyed. Electrons simply move from one atom to another, producing objects or regions with different charges. If you could count all the protons and all the electrons of all the atoms before and after charging an object, you would find that the numbers of protons and electrons do not change. Because charges are not created or destroyed, charge is said to be conserved.

✓ **Self-Check**

Plastic wrap clings to food containers because the wrap has a charge. Explain how plastic wrap becomes charged. (*See page 120 to check your answer.*)

Detecting Charge To determine if an object has a charge, you can use a device called an *electroscope*. An electroscope is a glass flask that contains a metal rod inserted through a rubber stopper. There are two metal leaves at the bottom of the rod. The leaves hang straight down when the electroscope is not charged but spread apart when it is charged, as shown in **Figure 6.**

Figure 6 *When an electroscope is charged, the metal leaves have the same charge and repel each other.*

Electrons from a negatively charged plastic ruler move to the electroscope and travel down the rod. The metal leaves become negatively charged and spread apart.

A positively charged glass rod attracts the electrons in the metal rod, causing the electrons to travel up the rod. The metal leaves become positively charged and spread apart.

SECTION REVIEW

1. Describe how an object is charged by friction.

2. Compare charging by conduction and induction.

3. **Inferring Conclusions** Suppose you are conducting experiments using an electroscope. You touch an object to the top of the electroscope, the metal leaves spread apart, and you determine that the object has a charge. However, you cannot determine the type of charge (positive or negative) the object has. Explain why not.

Moving Charges

Have you ever noticed that the cords that connect electrical devices to outlets are always covered in plastic, while the prongs that fit into the socket are always metal? Both plastic and metal are used to make electrical cords because they differ in their ability to transmit charges. In fact, most materials can be divided into two groups based on how easily charges travel through the material. The two groups are conductors and insulators.

Conductors A **conductor** is a material in which charges can move easily. Most metals are good conductors because some of the electrons in metals are free to move about. Copper, silver, aluminum, and mercury are good conductors.

Conductors are used to make wires and other objects that transmit charges. For example, the prongs on a lamp's cord are made of metal so that charges can move in the cord and transfer energy to light the lamp.

Not all conductors are metal. Household, or "tap," water conducts charges very well. Because tap water is a conductor, you can receive an electric shock from charges traveling in it. Therefore, you should avoid using electrical devices (such as the one in **Figure 7**) near water unless they are specially designed to be waterproof.

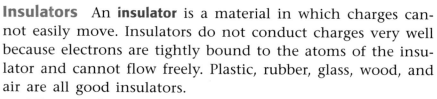

Figure 7 *Because tap water is a conductor, this hair dryer has a label that warns people not to use it near water.*

Insulators An **insulator** is a material in which charges cannot easily move. Insulators do not conduct charges very well because electrons are tightly bound to the atoms of the insulator and cannot flow freely. Plastic, rubber, glass, wood, and air are all good insulators.

Wires used to conduct electric charges are usually covered with an insulating material. The insulator prevents charges from leaving the wire and protects you from electric shock.

Static Electricity

After taking your clothes out of the dryer, you sometimes find clothing stuck together. When this happens, you might say that the clothes stick together because of static electricity. **Static electricity** is the buildup of electric charges on an object.

When something is *static,* it is not moving. The charges that create static electricity do not move away from the object they are stuck to. Therefore, the object remains charged. For example, your clothes are charged by friction as they rub against each other inside a dryer. Positive charges build up on some clothes, and negative charges build up on other clothes. Because clothing is an insulator, the charges stay on each piece of clothing, creating static electricity. You can see the result of static electricity in **Figure 8**.

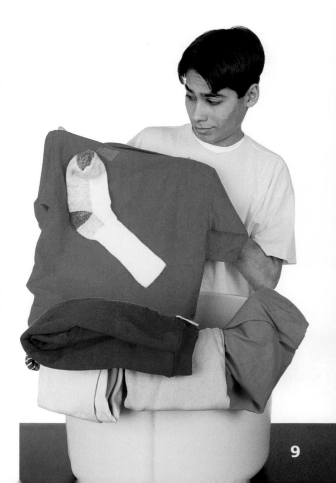

Figure 8 *Opposite charges on pieces of clothing are caused by static electricity. The clothes stick together because their charges attract each other.*

Electric Discharge Charges that build up as static electricity on an object eventually leave the object. The loss of static electricity as charges move off an object is called **electric discharge.** Sometimes electric discharge occurs slowly. For example, clothes stuck together by static electricity will eventually separate on their own because their electric charges are transferred to water molecules in the air over time.

Sometimes electric discharge occurs quickly and may be accompanied by a flash of light, a shock, or a cracking noise. For example, when you walk on a carpet with rubber-soled shoes, negative charges build up in your body. When you touch a metal doorknob, the negative charges in your body move quickly to the doorknob. Because the electric discharge happens quickly, you feel a shock.

Lightning

One of the most dramatic examples of electric discharge is lightning. Benjamin Franklin was the first to discover that lightning is a form of electricity. During a thunderstorm, Franklin flew a kite connected to a wire and successfully stored charge from a bolt of lightning. How does lightning form from a buildup of static electricity? **Figure 9** shows the answer.

Figure 9 How Lightning Forms

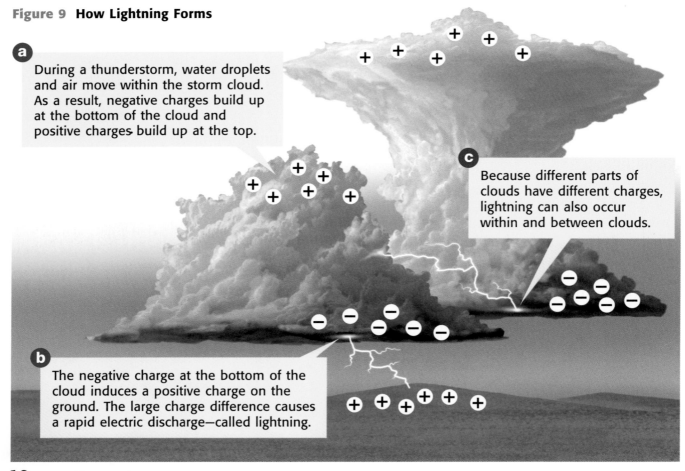

a During a thunderstorm, water droplets and air move within the storm cloud. As a result, negative charges build up at the bottom of the cloud and positive charges build up at the top.

c Because different parts of clouds have different charges, lightning can also occur within and between clouds.

b The negative charge at the bottom of the cloud induces a positive charge on the ground. The large charge difference causes a rapid electric discharge—called lightning.

Lightning Rods Benjamin Franklin also invented the lightning rod. A *lightning rod* is a pointed rod connected to the ground by a wire. Lightning usually strikes the highest point in a charged area because that point provides the easiest path for the charges to reach the ground. Therefore, lightning rods are always mounted so that they "stick out" and are the tallest point on a building, as shown in **Figure 10.**

Objects, such as a lightning rod, that are in contact with the Earth are *grounded*. Any object that is grounded provides a path for electric charges to travel to the Earth. Because the Earth is so large, it can give up or absorb electric charges without being damaged. When lightning strikes a lightning rod, the electric charges are carried safely to the Earth through the rod's wire. By directing the lightning's charge to the Earth, lightning rods prevent lightning damage to buildings.

Lightning Dangers Anything that sticks out in an area can provide a path for lightning. Trees and people in open areas are at risk of being struck by lightning. This is why it is particularly dangerous to be at the beach or on a golf course during a lightning storm. And standing under a tree during a storm is dangerous because the charge from lightning striking a tree can jump to your body.

Science
CONNECTION

Sprites and elves aren't just creatures in fairy tales! Read about how they are related to lightning on page 35.

Figure 10 *Lightning strikes the lightning rod rather than the building because the lightning rod is the tallest point on the building.*

SECTION REVIEW

1. What is static electricity? Give an example of static electricity.

2. How is the shock you receive from a metal doorknob similar to a bolt of lightning?

3. **Applying Concepts** When you use an electroscope, you touch a charged object to a metal rod that is held in place by a rubber stopper. Why is it important to touch the object to the metal rod and not to the rubber stopper?

internet**connect**

SC*L*INKS
NSTA

TOPIC: Static Electricity
GO TO: www.scilinks.org
*sci*LINKS NUMBER: HSTP405

Terms to Learn

cell   photocell
battery   thermocouple
potential difference

What You'll Do

◆ Explain how a cell produces an electric current.
◆ Describe how the potential difference is related to electric current.
◆ Describe how photocells and thermocouples produce electrical energy.

Electrical Energy

Imagine living without electrical energy. You could not watch television or listen to a portable radio, and you could not even turn on a light bulb to help you see in the dark! *Electrical energy*—the energy of electric charges—provides people with many comforts and conveniences. A flow of charges is called an *electric current*. Electric currents can be produced in many ways. One common way to produce electric current is through chemical reactions in a battery.

Batteries Are Included

In science, energy is defined as the ability to do work. Energy cannot be created or destroyed; it can only be converted into other types of energy. A **cell** is a device that produces an electric current by converting chemical energy into electrical energy. A **battery** also converts chemical energy into electrical energy and is made of several cells.

Parts of a Cell Every cell contains a mixture of chemicals that conducts a current; the mixture is called an *electrolyte* (ee LEK troh LIET). Chemical reactions in the electrolyte convert chemical energy into electrical energy. Every cell also contains a pair of electrodes made from two different conducting materials that are in contact with the electrolyte. An *electrode* (ee LEK TROHD) is the part of a cell through which charges enter or exit. **Figure 11** shows how a cell produces an electric current.

Figure 11 *This cell has a zinc electrode and a copper electrode dipped in a liquid electrolyte.*

Flow

a A chemical reaction leaves extra electrons on the zinc electrode. Therefore, the zinc electrode has a negative charge.

b A different chemical reaction causes electrons to be pulled off the copper electrode, making the copper electrode positively charged.

c If the electrodes are connected by a wire, charges will flow from the negative zinc electrode through the wire to the positive copper electrode, producing an electric current.

Types of Cells Cells are divided into two groups—wet cells and dry cells. Wet cells, such as the cell shown in Figure 11, contain liquid electrolytes. A car battery is made of several wet cells that use sulfuric acid as the electrolyte.

Dry cells work in a similar way, but dry cells contain electrolytes that are solid or pastelike. The cells used in portable radios and flashlights are examples of dry cells.

You can make your own cell by inserting strips of zinc and copper into a lemon. The electric current produced when the metal strips are connected is strong enough to power a small clock, as shown in **Figure 12.**

Figure 12 *This cell uses the juice of a lemon as an electrolyte and uses strips of zinc and copper as electrodes.*

Potatoes aren't just for eating anymore! Learn how to use a potato to produce an electric current on page 97 of the LabBook.

Bring On the Potential

So far you have learned that cells and batteries can produce electric currents. But why does the electric current exist between the two electrodes? The electric current exists because a chemical reaction causes a difference in charge between the two electrodes. The difference in charge means that an electric current—a flow of electric charges—can be produced by the cell to provide energy. The energy per unit charge is called the **potential difference** and is expressed in volts (V).

As long as there is a potential difference between the electrodes of a cell and there is a wire connecting them, charges will flow through the cell and the wire, creating an electric current. The current depends on the potential difference. The greater the potential difference is, the greater the current. **Figure 13** shows batteries and cells with different potential differences.

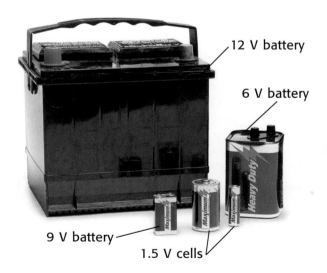

12 V battery

6 V battery

9 V battery

1.5 V cells

Figure 13 *Batteries are made with different potential differences. The potential difference of a battery depends on the number of cells it contains.*

Solar panel

Other Ways of Producing Electrical Energy

The conversion of chemical energy to electrical energy in batteries is not the only way electrical energy can be generated. Several technological devices have been developed to convert different types of energy into electrical energy for use every day. For example, generators convert kinetic energy into electrical energy. Two other devices that produce electrical energy are photocells and thermocouples.

Photocells Have you ever wondered how a solar-powered calculator works? If you look above the display of the calculator, you will see a dark strip called a solar panel. This panel is made of several photocells. A **photocell** is the part of a solar panel that converts light into electrical energy.

Photocells contain silicon atoms. When light strikes the photocell, electrons are ejected from the silicon atoms. If light continues to shine on the photocell, electrons will be steadily emitted. The ejected electrons are gathered into a wire to create an electric current.

Thermocouples Thermal energy can be converted to electrical energy by a **thermocouple.** A simple thermocouple is made by joining wires made of two different metals into a loop, as shown in **Figure 14.** The temperature difference within the loop causes charges to flow through the loop. Thermocouples are used to monitor the temperature of car engines, furnaces, and ovens.

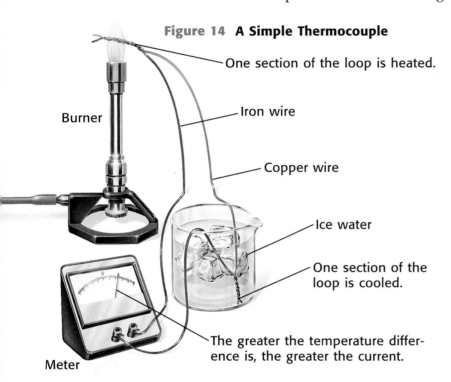

Figure 14 **A Simple Thermocouple**

One section of the loop is heated.

Burner

Iron wire

Copper wire

Ice water

One section of the loop is cooled.

The greater the temperature difference is, the greater the current.

Meter

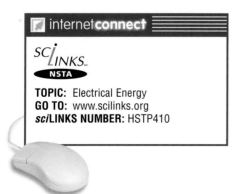
SECTION REVIEW

1. Name the parts of a cell, and explain how they work together to produce an electric current.

2. How do the currents produced by a 1.5 V flashlight cell and a 12 V car battery compare?

3. **Inferring Conclusions** Why do you think some solar calculators contain batteries?

Terms to Learn

current	resistance
voltage	electric power

What You'll Do

- Describe electric current.
- Identify the four factors that determine the resistance of an object.
- Explain how current, voltage, and resistance are related by Ohm's law.
- Describe how electric power is related to electrical energy.

Electric Current

So far you have read how electrical energy can be generated by a variety of methods. A battery produces electrical energy very effectively, but electric power plants provide most of the electrical energy used every day. In this section, you will learn more about electric current and about the electrical energy you use at home.

Current Revisited

In the previous section, you learned that electric current is a continuous flow of charge. **Current** is more precisely defined as the rate at which charge passes a given point. The higher the current is, the more charge passes the point each second. The unit for current is the *ampere* (A), which is sometimes called amp for short. In equations, the symbol for current is the letter *I*.

Charge Ahead! When you flip a light switch, the light comes on instantly. Many people think that happens because electrons travel through the wire at the speed of light. In fact, it's because an electric field is created at close to the speed of light.

Flipping the light switch sets up an electric field in the wire that connects to the light bulb. The electric field causes the free electrons in the wire to move, as illustrated in **Figure 15.** Because the electric field is created so quickly, the electrons start moving through the wire at practically the same instant. You can think of the electric field as a kind of command to the electrons to "Charge ahead!" The light comes on instantly because the electrons simultaneously obey this command. So the current that causes the bulb to light up is established very quickly, even though individual electrons move quite slowly. In fact, it may take a single electron over an hour to travel 1 m through a wire.

Figure 15 *Electrons moving in a wire make up current, a continuous flow of charge.*

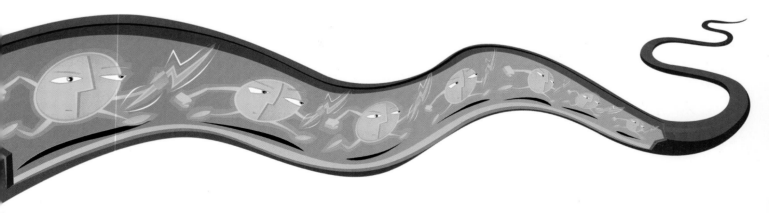

Let's See, AC/DC . . . There are two different types of electric current—direct current (DC) and alternating current (AC). In *direct current* the charges always flow in the same direction. In *alternating current* the charges continually switch from flowing in one direction to flowing in the reverse direction. **Figure 16** illustrates the difference between DC and AC.

The electric current produced by batteries and cells is DC, but the electric current from outlets in your home is AC. Both types of electric current can be used to provide electrical energy. For example, if you connect a flashlight bulb to a battery, the light bulb will light. You can light a household light bulb by attaching it to a lamp and turning the lamp switch on.

Alternating current is used in homes because it is more practical for transferring electrical energy. In the United States, the alternating current provided to households changes directions 120 times each second.

Figure 16 *Unlike DC, charges continually change direction in AC.*

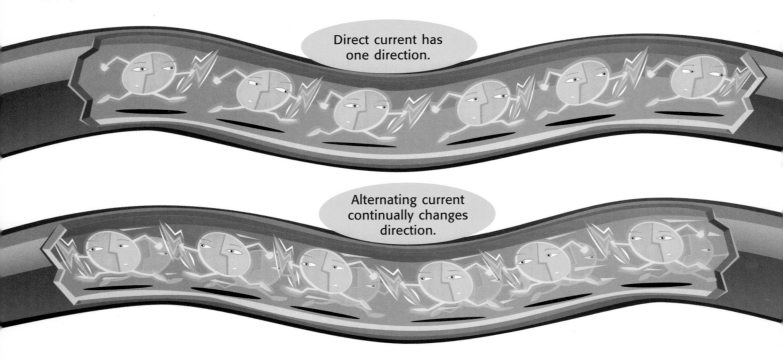

Direct current has one direction.

Alternating current continually changes direction.

Voltage

The current in a wire is determined by voltage. **Voltage** is the difference in energy per unit charge as a charge moves between two points in the path of a current. Voltage is another word for potential difference. Because voltage is the same as potential difference, voltage is expressed in volts. The symbol for voltage is the letter *V.* You can think of voltage as the amount of energy released as a charge moves between two points in the path of a current. The higher the voltage is, the more energy is released per charge. The current depends on the voltage. The greater the voltage is, the greater the current.

Voltage May Vary In the United States, electrical outlets usually supply a voltage of 120 V. Therefore, most electrical devices, such as televisions, toasters, lamps, and alarm clocks, are designed to run on 120 V. Devices that run on batteries or cells usually need a lower voltage. For example, a portable radio needs only 3 V. Compare this with the voltage created by the eel in **Figure 17**.

Figure 17 *An electric eel can create a voltage of more than 600 V!*

Resistance

In addition to voltage, resistance also determines the current in a wire. **Resistance** is the opposition to the flow of electric charge. Resistance is expressed in ohms (Ω, the Greek letter *omega*). In equations, the symbol for resistance is the letter *R*.

You can think of resistance as "electrical friction." The higher the resistance of a material is, the lower the current is in it. Therefore, as resistance increases, current decreases if the voltage is kept the same. An object's resistance varies depending on the object's material, thickness, length, and temperature.

Material Good conductors, such as copper, have low resistance. Poorer conductors, such as iron, have higher resistance. The resistance of insulators is so high that electric charges cannot flow in them.

Materials with low resistance are used to make wires and other objects that are used to transfer electrical energy from place to place. For example, most of the electrical cords in your house contain copper wires. However, it is sometimes helpful to use a material with high resistance, as shown in **Figure 18.**

Figure 18 *Tungsten light bulb filaments have a high resistance. This property causes electrical energy to be converted to light and thermal energy.*

Thickness and Length To understand how the thickness and length of a wire affect the wire's resistance, consider the model in **Figure 19.** The pipe filled with gravel represents a wire, and the water flowing through the pipe represents electric charges. This analogy illustrates that thick wires have less resistance than thin wires and that long wires have more resistance than short wires.

Figure 19 *Gravel in a pipe is like resistance in a wire. Just as gravel makes it more difficult for water to flow through the pipe, resistance makes it more difficult for electric charges to flow in a wire.*

A thick pipe has less resistance than a thin pipe because there are more spaces between pieces of gravel in a thick pipe for water to flow through.

A short pipe has less resistance than a long pipe because the water in a short pipe does not have to work its way around as many pieces of gravel.

Temperature Resistance also depends somewhat on temperature. In general, the resistance of metals increases as temperature increases. This happens because atoms move faster at higher temperatures and get in the way of the flowing electric charges.

If you cool certain materials to an extremely low temperature, resistance will drop to nearly 0 Ω. Materials in this state are called *superconductors*. A small superconductor is shown in **Figure 20.** Superconductors can be useful because very little energy is wasted when electric charges travel in them. However, so much energy is necessary to cool them that superconductors are not practical for everyday use.

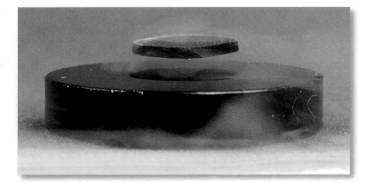

Figure 20 *One interesting property of superconductors is that they repel magnets. The superconductor in this photo is repelling the magnet so strongly that the magnet is floating.*

Ohm's Law: Putting It All Together

$$I = \frac{V}{R}$$

So far, you have learned about current, voltage, and resistance. But how are they related? A German school teacher named Georg Ohm asked this very question. He determined that the relationship between current (*I*), voltage (*V*), and resistance (*R*) could be expressed with the equation shown at right. This equation, which is known as *Ohm's law*, shows that the units of current, voltage, and resistance are related in the following way:

$$\text{amperes (A)} = \frac{\text{volts (V)}}{\text{ohms } (\Omega)}$$

You can use Ohm's law to find the current in a wire if you know the voltage applied and the resistance of the wire. For example, if a voltage of 30 V is applied to a wire with a resistance of 60 Ω, the current is as follows:

$$I = \frac{V}{R} = \frac{30 \text{ V}}{60 \text{ } \Omega} = 0.5 \text{ A}$$

Electric Power

You probably hear the word *power* used in different ways. Power can be used to mean force, strength, or energy. In science, power is the rate at which work is done. **Electric power** is the rate at which electrical energy is used to do work. The unit for power is the watt (W), and the symbol for power is the letter *P*. Electric power is calculated with the following equation:

$$\text{power} = \text{voltage} \times \text{current}, \quad \text{or} \quad P = V \times I$$

For the units:

$$\text{watts (W)} = \text{volts (V)} \times \text{amperes (A)}$$

÷ 5 ÷ Ω ∞ + Ω √ 9 ∞ ≤ Σ 2
+ ≤

MATH BREAK

Using Ohm's Law

You can use Ohm's law to find voltage or resistance:

$$V = I \times R \qquad R = \frac{V}{I}$$

If a 2 A current flows through a resistance of 12 Ω, the voltage is calculated as follows.

$$V = I \times R$$
$$V = 2 \text{ A} \times 12 \text{ } \Omega$$
$$V = 24 \text{ V}$$

Now It's Your Turn

1. Find the resistance of an object if a voltage of 10 V produces a current of 0.5 A.

2. Find the current produced if a voltage of 36 V is applied to a resistance of 4 Ω.

Watt Is a Power Rating?! If you have ever changed a light bulb, you are probably familiar with watts. Light bulbs have labels such as "60 W," "75 W," or "120 W." As electrical energy is supplied to a light bulb, the light bulb glows. As power increases, the bulb burns brighter because more electrical energy is converted to light energy. That is why a 120 W bulb burns brighter than a 60 W bulb.

Another common unit of power is the kilowatt (kW). One kilowatt is equal to 1,000 W. Kilowatts are used to express high values of power, such as the power needed to heat a house. The table shows the power ratings of some appliances you use every day.

Power Ratings of Household Appliances	
Appliance	**Power (W)**
Clothes dryer	4,000
Toaster	1,100
Hair dryer	1,000
Refrigerator/freezer	600
Color television	200
Radio	100
Clock	3

Measuring Electrical Energy

Electric power companies sell electrical energy to homes and businesses. Such companies determine how much a household or business has to pay based on power and time. For example, the amount of electrical energy used by a household depends on the power of the electrical devices in the house and how long those devices are on. The equation for electrical energy is as follows:

electrical energy = power × time,   or $E = P \times t$

✔ **Self-Check**

How much electrical energy is used by a color television that stays on for 2 hours? *(See page 120 to check your answer.)*

Measuring Household Energy Use Households use varying amounts of electrical energy during a day. Electric companies usually calculate electric energy by multiplying the power in kilowatts by the time in hours. The unit of electrical energy is usually kilowatt-hours (kWh). If a household used 2,000 W (2 kW) of power for 3 hours, it used 6 kWh of energy.

Electric power companies use electric meters such as the one shown at right to determine the number of kilowatt-hours of energy used by a household. Meters are often located outside houses and apartment buildings so someone from the power company can read them.

How to Save Energy

The amount of electrical energy used by an appliance depends on the power rating of the appliance and how long it is on. For example, a clock has a power rating of 3 W, and it is on 24 hours a day. Therefore, the clock uses 72 Wh (3 W × 24 hours), or 0.072 kWh, of energy a day. Using the information in the table on the previous page and an estimate of how long each appliance is on during a day, determine which appliances use the most energy and which use the least. Based on your findings, describe what you can do to use less energy.

SECTION REVIEW

1. What is electric current?

2. How does increasing the voltage affect the current?

3. How does an electric power company calculate electrical energy from electric power?

4. **Making Predictions** Which wire would have the lowest resistance: a long, thin iron wire at a high temperature or a short, thick copper wire at a low temperature?

5. **Doing Calculations** Use Ohm's law to find the voltage needed to produce a current of 3 A in a device with a resistance of 9 Ω.

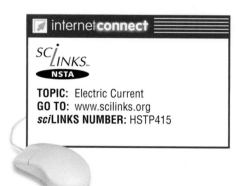

internet connect

*sci*LINKS
NSTA

TOPIC: Electric Current
GO TO: www.scilinks.org
*sci*LINKS NUMBER: HSTP415

What You'll Do

◆ Name the three essential parts of a circuit.
◆ Compare series circuits with parallel circuits.
◆ Explain how fuses and circuit breakers protect your home against short circuits and circuit overloads.

Electric Circuits

Imagine that you are lost in a forest. You need to find your way back to camp, where your friends are waiting for you. Unfortunately, there are no trails to follow, so you don't know which way to go. Just as you need a trail to follow in order to return to camp, electric charges need a path to follow in order to travel from an outlet or a battery to the device it provides energy to. A path that charges follow is called a circuit.

A circuit, however, is not exactly the same as a trail in a forest. A trail may begin in one place and end in another. But a circuit always begins and ends in the same place, forming a loop. Because a circuit forms a loop, it is said to be a closed path. So an electric **circuit** is a complete, closed path through which electric charges flow.

Parts of a Circuit

All circuits consist of an energy source, a load, and wires to connect the other parts together. A **load** is a device that uses electrical energy to do work. All loads offer some resistance to electric currents and cause the electrical energy to change into other forms of energy such as light energy or kinetic energy. **Figure 21** shows some examples of the different parts of a circuit.

Figure 21 Parts of a Circuit

a The energy source can be a battery, a photocell, a thermocouple, or an electric generator at a power plant.

b Wires connect the other parts of a circuit together. Wires are usually made of conducting materials with low resistance, such as copper.

c Examples of loads are light bulbs, appliances, televisions, and motors.

Opening and Closing a Circuit Sometimes a circuit also contains a switch. A switch is used to open and close a circuit. Usually a switch is made of two pieces of conducting material, one of which can be moved, as shown in **Figure 22.** For charges to flow through a circuit, the switch must be closed, or "turned on." If a switch is open, or "off," the loop of the circuit is broken and no charges can flow through the circuit. Light switches, power buttons on radios, and even the keys on calculators and computers work this way.

Biology
C O N N E C T I O N

Believe it or not, your body is controlled by a large electric circuit. Electrical impulses from your brain control all the muscles and organs in your body. The food you eat is the energy source for your body's circuit, your nerves are the wires, and your muscles and organs are the loads.

Figure 22 *You can turn a light bulb on and off by using a switch to close and open a circuit.*

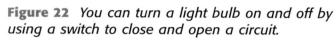

When the switch is **closed,** the two pieces of conducting material touch, allowing the electric charges to flow through the circuit.

When the switch is **open,** the gap between the two pieces of conducting material prevents the electric charges from traveling through the circuit.

✓ Self-Check

Is a microwave oven an example of a load? Why or why not? *(See page 120 to check your answer.)*

Types of Circuits

Look around the room for a moment, and count the number of objects that use electrical energy. You probably found several objects, such as lights, a clock, and maybe a computer. All of the objects you counted are loads in a large circuit that may include several rooms in the building. In fact, most circuits contain more than one load. The loads in a circuit can be connected in two different ways—in series or in parallel.

Series Circuits A **series circuit** is a circuit in which all parts are connected in a single loop. The charges traveling through a series circuit must flow through each part and can only follow one path. **Figure 23** shows an example of a series circuit.

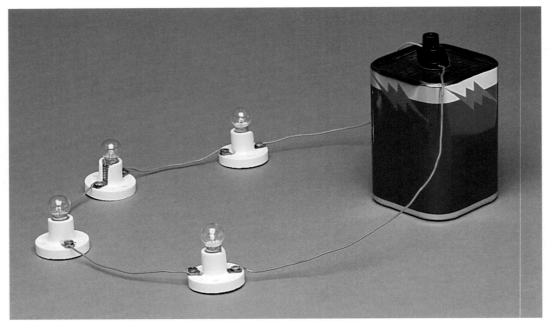

Figure 23 *The charges flow from the battery through each light bulb (load) and finally back to the battery.*

A Series of Circuits

1. Connect a **6 V battery** and **two flashlight bulbs** in a series circuit. Draw a picture of your circuit in your ScienceLog.

2. Add another **flashlight bulb** in series with the other two bulbs. How does the brightness of the light bulbs change?

3. Replace one of the light bulbs with a **burned-out light bulb.** What happens to the other lights in the circuit?

All the loads in a series circuit share the same current. Because the current in all the light bulbs in Figure 23 is the same, the light bulbs glow with the same brightness. However, if you add more light bulbs, the resistance of the entire circuit would increase and the current would decrease. Therefore, all the bulbs would be dimmer.

Uses for Series Circuits Some series circuits use a load as a switch. For example, the automatic door at the grocery store is operated by a series circuit with a motor that opens the door and a photoelectric device—an "electric eye"—that acts as an on-off switch. When no light hits the device, charges flow to the motor and the door opens.

For charges to flow in a series circuit, all the loads must be turned on and working. Charges pass through one load after another, in order, around the circuit. If one load is broken or missing, the other loads will not work. For example, if a television and a table lamp were connected in series and the lamp broke, your television would go off. This would be a problem at home, but it is useful in wiring bank alarms, some types of street lights, and certain computer circuits.

Parallel Circuits Think about what would happen if all the lights in your home were connected in series. If you needed a light on in your room, all the other lights in the house would have to be turned on too! Luckily, circuits in buildings are wired in parallel rather than in series. A **parallel circuit** is a circuit in which different loads are located on separate branches. Because there are separate branches, the charges travel through more than one path. **Figure 24** shows a parallel circuit.

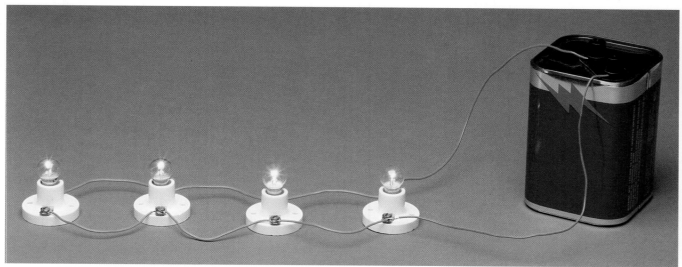

Figure 24 *The electric charges flow from the battery to each of the bulbs separately and then flow back to the battery.*

Unlike a series circuit, the loads in a parallel circuit do not have the same current in them. Instead, each load in a parallel circuit uses the same voltage. For example, the full voltage of the battery is applied to each bulb in Figure 24. As a result, each light bulb glows at full brightness, no matter how many bulbs are connected in parallel. You can connect loads that require different currents to the same parallel circuit. For example, you can connect a hair dryer, which requires a high current to operate, to the same circuit as a lamp, which requires less current.

Uses for Parallel Circuits In a parallel circuit, each branch of the circuit can function by itself. If one load is broken or missing, charges will still run through the other branches, and the loads on those branches will continue to work. In your home, each electrical outlet is usually on its own branch, with its own on-off switch. It would be inconvenient if each time a light bulb went out, your television or stereo stopped working. With parallel circuits, you can use one light or appliance at a time, even if another branch fails.

A Parallel Lab

1. Connect a **6 V battery** and **two flashlight bulbs** in a parallel circuit. Draw a picture of your circuit in your ScienceLog.

2. Add another **flashlight bulb** in parallel with the other two bulbs. How does the brightness of the light bulbs change?

3. Replace one of the light bulbs with a **burned-out light bulb.** What happens to the other lights in the circuit?

Household Circuits

In every home, several circuits connect lights, major appliances, and outlets throughout the building. Most household circuits are parallel circuits that can have several loads attached to them. The circuits branch out from a breaker box or a fuse box that acts as the "electrical headquarters" for the building. Each branch receives a standard voltage, which is 120 V in the United States.

Mayday! Circuit Failure! Broken wires or water can cause electrical appliances to short-circuit. A short circuit occurs when charges bypass the loads in the circuit. When the loads are bypassed, the resistance of the circuit drops, and the current in the circuit increases. If the current increases too much, it can produce enough thermal energy to start a fire. **Figure 25** shows how a short circuit might occur.

Figure 25 *If the insulating plastic around a cord is broken, the two wires inside can touch. The charges can then bypass the load and travel from one wire to the other.*

Circuits also may fail if they are overloaded. A circuit is overloaded when too many loads, or electrical devices, are attached to it. Each time you add a load to a parallel circuit, the entire circuit draws more current. If too many loads are attached to one circuit, the current increases to an unsafe level that can cause the temperature of the wires to increase and cause a fire. **Figure 26** shows a situation that can cause a circuit overload.

Figure 26 *Plugging too many devices into one outlet can cause a circuit to overload.*

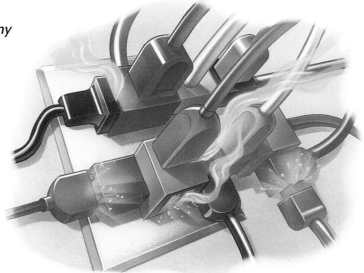

Circuit Safety

Because short circuits and circuit overloads can be so danger-ous, safety features are built into the circuits in your home. The two most commonly used safety devices are fuses and cir-cuit breakers, which are located in a fuse box or a breaker box.

Fuses A fuse contains a thin strip of metal through which the charges for a circuit flow. If the current in the circuit is too high, the metal in the fuse warms up and melts, as shown in **Figure 27.** A break or gap in the circuit is produced, and the charges stop flowing. This is referred to as blowing a fuse. After a fuse is blown, you must replace it with a new fuse in order for the charges to flow through the circuit again.

Figure 27 *The blown fuse on the left must be replaced with a new fuse, such as the one on the right.*

Circuit Breakers A circuit breaker is a switch that automat-ically opens if the current in the circuit is too high. If the current in a circuit is too high, a strip of metal in the cir-cuit breaker warms up and bends away from the wires in the circuit. A break in the circuit results. Open circuit breakers can be closed easily by flipping a switch inside the breaker box once the problem has been corrected.

A device that acts like a miniature circuit breaker is a ground fault circuit interrupter (GFCI). A GFCI, like the one shown in **Figure 28,** provides pro-tection by comparing the current in one side of an outlet with the current in the other side. If there is even a small difference, the GFCI opens the circuit. To close the circuit, you must push the RESET button.

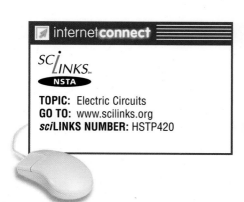

Figure 28 *GFCI devices are usually found on outlets in bathrooms and kitchens to protect you from electric shock.*

SECTION REVIEW

1. Name and describe the three essential parts of a circuit.

2. Why are switches useful in a circuit?

3. What is the difference between series and parallel circuits?

4. How do fuses and circuit breakers protect your home against electrical fires?

5. **Developing Hypotheses** Whenever you turn on the portable heater in your room, the circuit breaker for the circuit in your room opens and all the lights go out. Propose two possible reasons for why this occurs.

internetconnect

SC*i*LINKS
NSTA

TOPIC: Electric Circuits
GO TO: www.scilinks.org
*sci*LINKS NUMBER: HSTP420

Skill Builder Lab

Circuitry 101

In this lab, you will construct both a series circuit and a parallel circuit. You will use an ammeter to measure current and a voltmeter to measure voltage.

MATERIALS

- power source—dry cell(s)
- switch
- 3 light bulb holders
- 3 light bulbs
- insulated wire, cut into 15 cm lengths with both ends stripped
- ammeter
- voltmeter

Part A: Series Circuit

Procedure

1 Construct a series circuit with a power source, a switch, and three light bulbs.
Caution: Always leave the switch open when constructing or changing the circuit. Close the switch only when testing or taking a reading.

2 Draw your circuit in your ScienceLog.

3 Test your circuit. Do all three bulbs light up? Are they all the same brightness? What happens if you carefully unscrew one light bulb? Does it make any difference which bulb you unscrew? Record your observations in your ScienceLog.

4 Connect the ammeter between the power source and the switch. Close the switch, and record the current on your diagram in your ScienceLog. Use a label to show where you measured the current and what the value was.

5 Reconnect the circuit. Place the ammeter between the first and second bulbs. Record the current, as you did in step 4.

6 Move the ammeter. Place it between the second and third bulbs. Record the current again. Remove the ammeter from the circuit.

7 Connect the voltmeter to the two ends of the power source. Label the voltage on your diagram.

8 Use the voltmeter to measure the voltage across each bulb. Label the voltage across each bulb on your diagram.

Part B: Parallel Circuit

Procedure

9 Take apart your series circuit. Reassemble the same power source, switch, and three light bulbs so that the bulbs are wired in parallel. (Note: The switch must remain in series with the power source to be able to control the whole circuit.)

10 Draw a diagram of your parallel circuit in your ScienceLog.

11 Test your circuit, and record your observations, as you did in step 3.

12 Connect the ammeter between the power source and the switch. Record the reading on your diagram.

13 Reconnect the circuit so that the ammeter is right next to one of the three bulbs. Record the current on your diagram.

14 Repeat step 13 for the remaining bulbs. Remove the ammeter from your circuit.

15 Connect the voltmeter to the two ends of the power source. Record this voltage.

16 Measure and record the voltage across each light bulb.

Analysis: Parts A and B

17 Was the current the same everywhere in the series circuit? Was it the same everywhere in the parallel circuit?

18 For each circuit, compare the voltage across each light bulb with the voltage across the power source.

19 What is the relationship between the voltage across the power source and the voltages across the light bulbs in a series circuit?

20 Was the total resistance for both circuits the same? Explain your answer.

21 Why did the bulbs differ in brightness?

22 Consider your results. What do you think might happen if too many things are plugged into the same series circuit? the same parallel circuit?

23 Compare your results with others in the class.

Chapter Highlights

SECTION 1

Vocabulary

law of electric charges (*p. 5*)

electric force (*p. 5*)

conduction (*p. 7*)

induction (*p. 7*)

conductor (*p. 9*)

insulator (*p. 9*)

static electricity (*p. 9*)

electric discharge (*p. 10*)

Section Notes

- The law of electric charges states that like charges repel and opposite charges attract.

- The electric force varies depending on the size of the charges exerting the force and the distance between them.

- Objects become charged when they gain or lose electrons. Objects may become charged by friction, conduction, or induction.

- Charges are not created or destroyed and are said to be conserved.

- An electroscope can be used to detect charges.

- Charges move easily in conductors but do not move easily in insulators.

- Static electricity is the buildup of electric charges on an object. Static electricity is lost through electric discharge. Lightning is a form of electric discharge.

- Lightning rods work by directing the electric charge carried by lightning safely to the Earth.

Labs

Stop the Static Electricity! (*p. 96*)

SECTION 2

Vocabulary

cell (*p. 12*)

battery (*p. 12*)

potential difference (*p. 13*)

photocell (*p. 14*)

thermocouple (*p. 14*)

Section Notes

- Batteries are made of cells that convert chemical energy to electrical energy.

- Electric currents can be produced when there is a potential difference.

- Photocells and thermocouples are devices used to produce electrical energy.

Labs

Potato Power (*p. 97*)

☑ Skills Check

Math Concepts

OHM'S LAW Ohm's law, shown on page 19, describes the relationship between current, voltage, and resistance. If you know two of the values, you can always calculate the third. For example, the current in a wire with a resistance of 4 Ω produced by a voltage of 12 V is calculated as follows:

$$I = \frac{V}{R} = \frac{12 \text{ V}}{4 \text{ Ω}} = 3 \text{ A}$$

Visual Understanding

SERIES AND PARALLEL CIRCUITS There are two types of circuits— series and parallel. The charges in a series circuit follow only one path, but the charges in a parallel circuit follow more than one path. Look at Figures 23 and 24 on pages 24–25 to review series and parallel circuits.

SECTION 3

Vocabulary

current *(p. 15)*

voltage *(p. 16)*

resistance *(p. 17)*

electric power *(p. 19)*

Section Notes

- Electric current is a continuous flow of charge caused by the motion of electrons.

- Voltage is the same as potential difference. As voltage increases, current increases.

- An object's resistance varies depending on the object's material, thickness, length, and temperature. As resistance increases, current decreases.

- Ohm's law describes the relationship between current, resistance, and voltage.

- Electric power is the rate at which electrical energy does work. It is expressed in watts or kilowatts.

- Electrical energy is electric power multiplied by time. It is usually expressed in kilowatt-hours.

SECTION 4

Vocabulary

circuit *(p. 22)*

load *(p. 22)*

series circuit *(p. 24)*

parallel circuit *(p. 25)*

Section Notes

- Circuits consist of an energy source, a load, wires, and sometimes a switch.

- All parts of a series circuit are connected in a single loop.

- The loads in a parallel circuit are on separate branches.

- Circuits can fail because of a short circuit or circuit overload.

- Fuses or circuit breakers protect your home against circuit failure.

---

internet connect

GO TO: go.hrw.com

Visit the **HRW** Web site for a variety of learning tools related to this chapter. Just type in the keyword:

KEYWORD: HSTELE

GO TO: www.scilinks.org

Visit the **National Science Teachers Association** on-line Web site for Internet resources related to this chapter. Just type in the *sci*LINKS number for more information about the topic:

TOPIC: Static Electricity   *sci*LINKS NUMBER: HSTP405

TOPIC: Electrical Energy   *sci*LINKS NUMBER: HSTP410

TOPIC: Electric Current   *sci*LINKS NUMBER: HSTP415

TOPIC: Electric Circuits   *sci*LINKS NUMBER: HSTP420

Chapter Review

To complete the following sentences, choose the correct term from each pair of terms listed below:

1. A __?__ converts chemical energy into electrical energy. (*battery* or *photocell*)

2. Charges flow easily in a(n) __?__. (*insulator* or *conductor*)

3. __?__ is the opposition to the flow of electric charge. (*Resistance* or *Electric power*)

4. A __?__ is a complete, closed path through which charges flow. (*load* or *circuit*)

5. Lightning is a form of __?__. (*static electricity* or *electric discharge*)

UNDERSTANDING CONCEPTS

Multiple Choice

6. If two charges repel each other, the two charges must be
   a. positive and positive.
   b. positive and negative.
   c. negative and negative.
   d. Either (a) or (c)

7. A device that can convert chemical energy to electrical energy is a
   a. lightning rod.
   b. cell.
   c. light bulb.
   d. All of the above

8. Which of the following wires has the lowest resistance?
   a. a short, thick copper wire at 25°C
   b. a long, thick copper wire at 35°C
   c. a long, thin copper wire at 35°C
   d. a short, thick iron wire at 25°C

9. An object becomes charged when the atoms in the object gain or lose
   a. protons.   c. electrons.
   b. neutrons.   d. All of the above

10. A device used to protect buildings from electrical fires is a(n)
    a. electric meter.   c. fuse.
    b. circuit breaker. d. Both (b) and (c)

11. In order to produce a current from a cell, the electrodes of the cell must
    a. have a potential difference.
    b. be in a liquid.
    c. be exposed to light.
    d. be at two different temperatures.

12. What type of current comes from the outlets in your home?
    a. direct current   c. electric discharge
    b. alternating current   d. static electricity

Short Answer

13. List and describe the three essential parts of a circuit.

14. Name the two factors that affect the strength of electric force, and explain how they affect electric force.

15. Describe how direct current differs from alternating current.

Concept Mapping

16. Use the following terms to create a concept map: electric current, battery, charges, photocell, thermocouple, circuit, parallel circuit, series circuit.

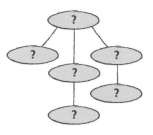

CRITICAL THINKING AND PROBLEM SOLVING

17. Your science classroom was rewired over the weekend. On Monday, you notice that the electrician may have made a mistake. In order for the fish-tank bubbler to work, the lights in the room must be on. And if you want to use the computer, you must turn on the overhead projector. Describe what mistake the electrician made with the circuits in your classroom.

18. You can make a cell using an apple, a strip of copper, and a strip of silver. Explain how you would construct the cell, and identify the parts of the cell. What type of cell is formed? Explain your answer.

19. Your friend shows you a magic trick. She rubs a plastic comb with a piece of silk and holds the comb close to a stream of water. When the comb is close to the water, the water bends toward the comb. Explain how this trick works. (Hint: Think about how objects become charged.)

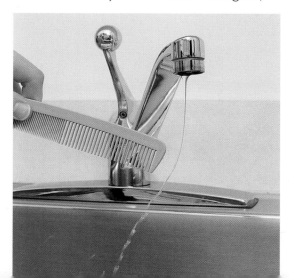

MATH IN SCIENCE

Use Ohm's law to solve the following problems:

20. What voltage is needed to produce a 6 A current through a resistance of 3 Ω?

21. Find the current produced when a voltage of 60 V is applied to a resistance of 15 Ω.

22. What is the resistance of an object if a voltage of 40 V produces a current of 5 A?

INTERPRETING GRAPHICS

23. Classify the objects in the photograph below as conductors or insulators.

Reading Check-up

Take a minute to review your answers to the Pre-Reading Questions found at the bottom of page 2. Have your answers changed? If necessary, revise your answers based on what you have learned since you began this chapter.

Science, Technology, and Society

Riding the Electric Rails

For more than 100 years, the trolley, or streetcar, was a popular way to travel around a city. Then, beginning in the 1950s, most cities ripped up their trolley tracks to make way for automobiles. Today, trolleys are making a comeback around the world.

From Horse Power to Electric Power

In 1832, the first trolleys, called *horsecars,* were pulled by horses through the streets of New York. Soon horsecars were used in most large cities in the United States. However, using horses for power presented several problems. Among other things, the horses were slow and required special attention and constant care. So inventors began looking for other sources of power.

In 1888, Frank J. Sprague developed a way to operate trolleys with electrical energy. These electric trolleys ran on a metal track and were connected by a pole to an overhead power line. Electric charges flowed down the pole to motors in the trolley. A wheel at the top of the pole, called a *shoe,* rolled along the power line, allowing the trolley to move along its track without losing contact with its power source. The charges passed through the motor and then returned to a power generator by way of the metal track.

Taking It to the Streets

By World War I, more than 40,000 km of electric-trolley tracks were in use in the United States. The trolley's popularity helped shape American cities because businesses were built along the trolley lines. But competition from cars and buses grew over the next decade, and many trolley lines were abandoned.

By the 1980s, nearly all of the trolley lines had been shut down. But by then, people were looking for new ways to cut down on the pollution, noise, and traffic problems caused by auto-

▲ *The horsecar was a popular mode of travel in many cities during the early 1900s.*

mobiles and buses. Trolleys provided one possible solution. Because they run on electrical energy, they create little pollution, and because many people can ride on a single trolley, they cut down on traffic.

Today, a new form of trolley is being used in a number of major cities. These light-rail transit vehicles are quieter, faster, and more economical than the older trolleys. They usually run on rails alongside the road and contain new systems, such as automated brakes and speed controls.

Think About It!

▶ Because trolleys operate on electrical energy, does this mean that they don't create any pollution? Explain your answer.

▲ *Many cities across the country now use light-rail systems for public transportation.*

Sprites and Elves

Imagine you are a pilot flying a plane on a moonless night. About 80 km away, you notice a powerful thunderstorm and see the lightning move *between* the clouds and the Earth. This makes sense because you know that all weather activity takes place in the lowest layer of Earth's atmosphere, which is called the troposphere. But all of a sudden, a ghostly red glow stretches many kilometers *above* the storm clouds and *into* the stratosphere!

Capturing Sprites

In 1989, scientists at the University of Minnesota followed the trail of many such reports. They captured the first image of this strange, red-glowing lightning using a video camera. Since then, photographs from space shuttles, airplanes, telescopes, and observers on the ground have identified several types of wispy electrical glows. Two of these types were named sprites and elves because, like the mythical creatures, they last only a few thousandths of a second and disappear just as the eye begins to see them.

Photographs show that sprites and elves occur only when ordinary lightning is discharged from a cloud. Sprites are very large, extending from the cloud tops at an altitude of about 15 km to as high as 95 km. They are up to 50 km wide. Elves are expanding disks of red light, probably caused by an electromagnetic pulse from lightning or sprites. Elves can be 200 km across, and they appear at altitudes above 90 km.

What Took So Long?

It is likely that sprites and elves have been occurring for thousands of years but went unrecorded. This is because they are produced with only about 1 percent of lightning flashes. They also last for a short period of time and are very faint. Since they occur above thunderclouds, where few people can see, observers are more often distracted by the brighter lightning below.

▲ *Sprites (left) and elves (right) are strange electric discharges in the atmosphere.*

Still, scientists are not surprised to learn that electric discharges extend up from clouds. There is a large potential difference between thunderclouds and the ionosphere, an atmospheric level above the clouds. The ionosphere is electrically conductive and provides a path for these electric discharges.

Search and Find

► Would you like to find sprites on your own? (Elves disappear too quickly.) Go with an adult, avoid being out in a thunderstorm, and remember:

● It must be completely dark, and your eyes must adjust to the total darkness.
● Viewing is best when a large thunderstorm is 48 to 97 km away, with no clouds in between.
● Block out the lightning below the clouds with dark paper so that you can still see above the clouds.
● Be patient.

Report sightings to a university geophysical department. Scientists need more information to fully understand how these discharges affect the chemical and electrical workings of our atmosphere.

Electromagnetism

Pre-Reading
Questions

1. What are the properties
of magnets?

2. How does electricity
produce magnetism?

3. How does magnetism
produce electricity?

ELECTRIC HIGH SPEED TRAINS

Meet the Eurostar, an electric passenger train that runs at speeds up to 298 kilometers per hour (186 mph). The Eurostar railway connects France, England, and Belgium, traveling through the "Chunnel," a 50-kilometer (30-mile)-long tunnel under the English Channel. The train gets its electrical power either through a third rail beneath the train or through overhead wires. In this chapter, you will learn how electricity and magnetic force are related, how electric motors work, and how electrical power is generated.

MAGNETIC ATTRACTION

In this activity, you will investigate ways you can use a magnet to lift steel.

Procedure

1. Place **5 steel paper clips** on your desk. Touch the clips with an **unmagnetized iron nail.** Lift the nail and record the number of clips that stick to the nail.

2. Touch the clips with the end of a **strong bar magnet.** Record the number of clips that stick to it.

3. While holding the magnet against the head of the nail, touch the tip of the nail to the paper clips. Count the number of paper clips that stick to the nail.

4. Remove the magnet from the end of the nail, and observe what happens. Record the number of paper clips you counted in step 3 and your observations from step 4.

5. Drag one end of the bar magnet 50 times down the nail. Drag the magnet in only one direction.

6. Set the magnet aside. Touch the nail to the clips. Record the number of clips that stick to it.

Analysis

7. What caused the difference between the number of paper clips you picked up in step 1 and step 3?

8. What effect did the magnet have on the nail in step 5?

What You'll Do

◆ Describe the force between two magnetic poles.

◆ Explain why some materials are magnetic and some are not.

◆ Describe four different categories of magnets.

◆ Give two examples of the effect of Earth's magnetic field.

Magnets and Magnetism

You've probably seen magnets like the ones at right and below, stuck to a refrigerator door. These magnets might have been used to hold up notes or pictures or might have been used just for decoration. If you have ever played with magnets, you know that they stick to each other and to some types of metals. You also know that magnets can stick to objects without directly touching them—like when one is used to hold a piece of paper to a refrigerator door. How do magnets work? Read on to find out.

Properties of Magnets

More than 2,000 years ago, the Greeks discovered a mineral that attracted objects containing iron. Because this mineral was found in a part of Turkey called Magnesia, the Greeks called it magnetite. Today any material that attracts iron or materials containing iron is called a **magnet.** All magnets have certain properties. For example, all magnets have two poles, exert forces, and are surrounded by a magnetic field.

Magnetic Poles The magnetic effects of a magnet are not evenly distributed throughout the magnet. For example, if you dip a bar magnet into a box of paper clips, you will find that most of the paper clips stick to the ends of the bar, as shown in **Figure 1.** As you can see, the magnetic effects are strongest near the ends of the bar magnet. The parts of a magnet where the magnetic effects are strongest are called **poles.**

Figure 1 *More paper clips stick to the ends, or poles, of a magnet because that's where the magnetic effects are strongest.*

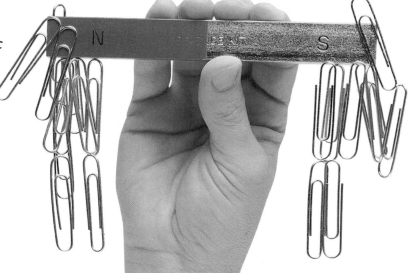

North and South If you attach a magnet to a string so that the magnet is free to rotate, you will see that one end of the magnet always ends up pointing to the north, as shown in **Figure 2.** The pole of a magnet that points to the north is called the magnet's north pole. The opposite end of the magnet points to the south and is therefore called the magnet's south pole. Magnetic poles always occur in pairs; you will never find a magnet with only a north pole or only a south pole.

Figure 2 *The needle in a compass is a magnet that is free to rotate.*

Magnetic Forces When you bring two magnets close together, the magnets each exert a force that can either push the magnets apart or pull them together. The force of repulsion or attraction between the poles of magnets is called the **magnetic force.** The magnetic force between a pair of magnets depends on how the poles of the magnets line up, as shown in **Figure 3.** As you can see, magnetic poles are similar to electric charges in that like poles repel and opposite poles attract.

Figure 3 **Magnetic Force Between Magnets**

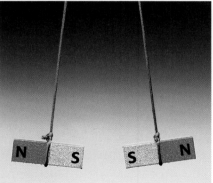

If you hold the north poles of two magnets close together, the magnetic force will push the magnets apart. The same is true if you hold the south poles close together.

If you hold the north pole of one magnet close to the south pole of another magnet, the magnetic force will pull the magnets together.

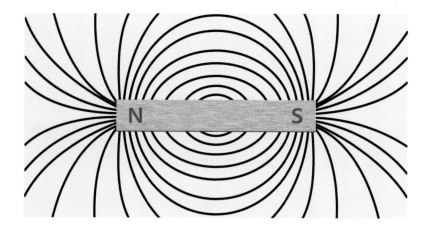

Magnetic Fields A *magnetic field* exists in the region around a magnet in which magnetic forces can act. The shape of a magnetic field can be shown with lines drawn from the north pole of a magnet to the south pole, as shown in **Figure 4.** These lines map the strength of magnetic force and are called magnetic field lines. The closer together the field lines are, the stronger the magnetic field is. Magnetic field lines around a magnet are closest together at the poles, showing that the magnetic force is strongest at these two places.

Figure 4 *Magnetic field lines show the shape of a magnetic field around a magnet. You can model magnetic field lines by sprinkling iron filings around a magnet.*

What Makes Materials Magnetic?

Some materials are magnetic, and some are not. For example, a magnet can pick up objects such as paper clips and iron nails, but it cannot pick up paper, plastic, pennies, or aluminum foil. What causes the difference? Whether a material is magnetic depends on the atoms in the material.

Grazing cows sometimes eat pieces of metal that have fallen on the ground. To protect their cows, ranchers have them swallow special cow magnets. These magnets stay in one of the cow's stomachs and attract any metal objects containing iron that the cow eats. This keeps the metal from traveling through the rest of the cow's digestive system.

Atoms and Domains All matter is composed of atoms. In the atoms, electrons are the negatively charged particles that move around the nucleus. Moving electrons produce magnetic fields that can give an atom a north and a south pole. In most materials, such as copper and aluminum, the magnetic fields of the individual atoms cancel each other out, so the materials aren't magnetic. However, in materials like iron, nickel, and cobalt, the atoms group together in tiny regions called *domains*. The atoms in a domain are arranged so that the north and south poles of all the atoms line up and create a strong magnetic field. Domains are like tiny magnets of different sizes within an object. **Figure 5,** on the next page, shows how domains affect the magnetic properties of an object.

Figure 5 *The arrangement of domains in an object determines whether the object is magnetic.*

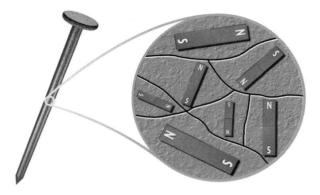

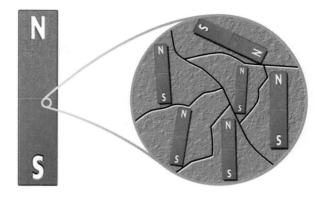

If the domains in an object are randomly arranged, the magnetic fields of the individual domains cancel each other out, and the object overall has no magnetic properties.

If most of the domains in an object are aligned, the magnetic fields of the individual domains combine to make the whole object magnetic.

Losing Alignment The domains of a magnet may not always stay aligned. Dropping a magnet or striking it too hard can jostle the domains out of alignment, causing the magnet to lose its magnetic properties. Increasing the temperature of a magnet can also demagnetize it. At higher temperatures, atoms in the magnet vibrate faster and lose their alignment within the domains.

Making Magnets A magnet can be made from an unmagnetized object made of iron, cobalt, or nickel by aligning the domains in the object. For example, you can magnetize an iron nail if you rub it in one direction with one pole of a magnet. The magnetic field of the magnet will cause the domains in the nail to rotate and align with the domains in the magnet. As more domains become aligned, the overall magnetic field of the nail will strengthen, and the nail will become a magnet, as shown in **Figure 6.**

The process of making a magnet also explains how a magnet can pick up an unmagnetized object, such as a paper clip. When you hold a magnet close to a paper clip, the magnetic field of the magnet causes the domains in the paper clip to align slightly, creating a temporary magnet. The domains align such that the north pole of the paper clip points toward the south pole of the magnet. The paper clip is therefore attracted to the magnet. The domains of the paper clip return to a random arrangement after the magnet is removed.

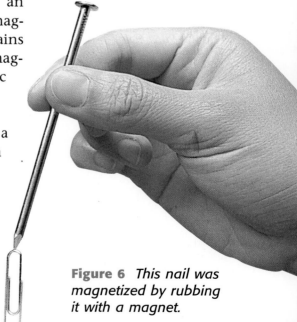

Figure 6 *This nail was magnetized by rubbing it with a magnet.*

Half a Magnet? What do you think would happen if you cut a magnet in half? You might predict that you would end up with one north-pole piece and one south-pole piece. But that's not what happens. When you cut a magnet in half, you end up with two magnets, each with its own north pole and south pole, as shown in **Figure 7.** Each domain within a magnet is like a tiny magnet with a north and south pole, so even the smallest pieces of a magnet have two poles.

Figure 7 *If you cut a magnet into pieces, each piece will still be a magnet with two poles.*

SECTION REVIEW

1. Name three properties of magnets.

2. Why are some iron objects magnetic and others not magnetic?

3. **Applying Concepts** Suppose you have two bar magnets. One has its north and south poles marked, but the other one does not. Describe how you could use the first magnet to identify the poles of the second magnet.

Figure 8 *Magnetite attracts objects containing iron and is a ferromagnet.*

Types of Magnets

There are different ways to describe magnets. The magnets you may be most familiar with are those made of iron, nickel, cobalt, or alloys of those metals. Magnets made with these metals have strong magnetic properties and are called *ferromagnets.* The mineral magnetite, which you read about at the beginning of this section and which is shown in **Figure 8,** is an example of a naturally occurring ferromagnet. Another type of magnet is the *electromagnet.* An electromagnet is a magnet, usually with an iron core, produced by an electric current. You will learn more about electromagnets in the next section.

Temporary and Permanent Magnets Magnets can also be described as temporary magnets or permanent magnets. *Temporary magnets* are made from materials that are easy to magnetize but tend to lose their magnetization easily. Soft iron (iron that is not mixed with any other materials) can be made into temporary magnets. *Permanent magnets,* on the other hand, are difficult to magnetize but tend to retain their magnetic properties better. Strong permanent magnets are made with alnico (AL ni кон)—an alloy of aluminum, nickel, and cobalt.

Earth as a Magnet

Recall that one end of every magnet points to the north if the magnet is allowed to rotate freely. For more than 2,000 years, travelers and explorers have relied on this to help them navigate. In fact, you take advantage of this property any time you use a compass, because a compass contains a freely rotating magnet. But why do magnets point to the north? Read on to find out.

One Giant Magnet In 1600, an English physician named William Gilbert suggested that magnets point to the north because Earth itself is one giant magnet. In fact, Earth behaves as if it has a bar magnet running through its center. The poles of this imaginary magnet are located near Earth's geographic poles, as shown in **Figure 9**.

QuickLab

Model of Earth's Magnetic Field

1. On a **sheet of butcher paper,** draw a circle with a diameter larger than a bar magnet. This represents the surface of the Earth. Label Earth's North and South Poles.

2. Place a **bar magnet** under the butcher paper and line it up with the poles.

3. Sprinkle some **iron filings** lightly around the perimeter of the circle. In your ScienceLog, describe and sketch the pattern you see.

Figure 9 *The magnetic poles of Earth are close to—but not the same as—the geographic poles.*

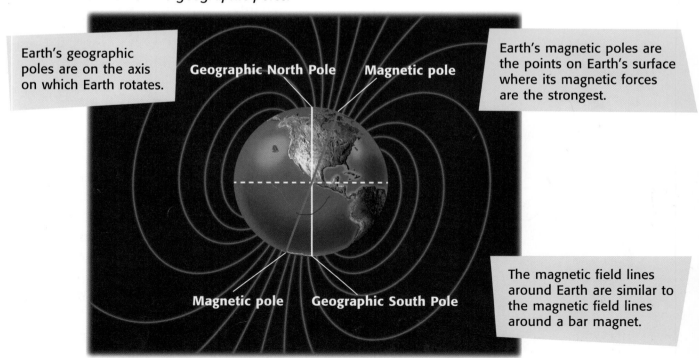

Earth's geographic poles are on the axis on which Earth rotates.

Geographic North Pole   Magnetic pole

Earth's magnetic poles are the points on Earth's surface where its magnetic forces are the strongest.

Magnetic pole   Geographic South Pole

The magnetic field lines around Earth are similar to the magnetic field lines around a bar magnet.

Scientists think that birds may use the Earth's magnetic field to help them navigate. Tiny pieces of magnetite have been found in the brains of birds, which could help them sense which direction is north as they fly.

North or South? Try this simple experiment. Place a compass on a bar magnet that has its north and south poles marked. Which pole of the magnet did the marked end of the needle of the compass point to? If your compass is working properly, the marked end should have pointed to the south pole of the magnet, as shown in **Figure 10.** Does that surprise you? Think about what you have already learned about magnets.

Figure 10 *The marked end of a compass needle always points to the south pole of a magnet.*

One property of magnets is that opposite poles attract each other. That means that the north pole of one magnet is attracted to the south pole of another magnet. A compass needle is a small magnet, and the tip that points to the north is the needle's north pole. Therefore, the point of a compass needle will be attracted to the south pole of a bar magnet.

North Is South! So why does the needle of a compass point north? The answer is that the magnetic pole of Earth that is closest to the geographic North Pole is actually a magnetic *south* pole! So a compass needle points to the north because its north pole is attracted to a very large magnetic south pole.

Figure 11 *The Earth acts like a giant magnet.*

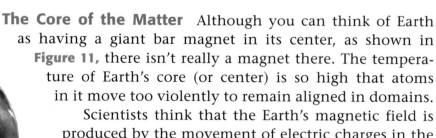

The Core of the Matter Although you can think of Earth as having a giant bar magnet in its center, as shown in **Figure 11,** there isn't really a magnet there. The temperature of Earth's core (or center) is so high that atoms in it move too violently to remain aligned in domains. Scientists think that the Earth's magnetic field is produced by the movement of electric charges in the Earth's core. The Earth's core is made mostly of iron and nickel. The inner core is solid because it is under such great pressure. In the outer core, the pressure is less and the metals are in a liquid state. As Earth rotates, the liquid in the core flows and causes electric charges to move, creating a magnetic field.

A Magnetic Light Show One of the most spectacular effects caused by the Earth's magnetic field is a curtain of light called an *aurora,* like the one shown in **Figure 12.** An aurora is formed when charged particles from the sun interact with oxygen and nitrogen atoms in Earth's atmosphere. When charged particles from the sun strike these atoms, the atoms emit light of different colors.

Figure 12 *The photo at left shows what an aurora looks like from the ground.*

Earth's magnetic field acts like a barrier to most charged particles from the sun, so the particles cannot strike the atmosphere in most places. But because Earth's magnetic field bends inward at the magnetic poles, the charged particles can crash into the atmosphere at and near the poles. Therefore, auroras are most often seen in areas near the north and south magnetic poles. Auroras seen near the north magnetic pole are called aurora borealis (ah ROHR uh BOHR ee AL is), the northern lights, and auroras seen near the south magnetic pole are called aurora australis (ah ROHR uh ah STRAY lis), the southern lights.

Science CONNECTION

Auroras are a result of geomagnetic storms. Read more about these storms on page 64.

SECTION REVIEW

1. Name the metals used to make ferromagnets.

2. How are temporary magnets different from permanent magnets?

3. **Applying Concepts** Why are auroras more commonly seen in places like Alaska and Australia than in places like Florida and Mexico?

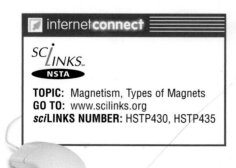

internet connect

*sci*LINKS
NSTA

TOPIC: Magnetism, Types of Magnets
GO TO: www.scilinks.org
*sci*LINKS NUMBER: HSTP430, HSTP435

What You'll Do

- Identify the relationship between an electric current and a magnetic field.
- Compare solenoids, electromagnets, and magnets.
- Describe how electromagnetism is involved in the operation of doorbells, electric motors, and galvanometers.

Magnetism from Electricity

Most of the trains you see roll on wheels on top of a track. But engineers have developed trains that have no wheels and actually float above the track. These trains are able to levitate because of magnetic forces between the track and the train cars. Such trains are called maglev trains. The name *maglev* is short for magnetic levitation. To levitate, maglev trains use a type of magnet called an electromagnet, which can produce a strong magnetic field. In this section you will learn how electricity and magnetism are related and how electromagnets are made.

The Discovery of Electromagnetism

Danish physicist Hans Christian Oersted discovered the relationship between electricity and magnetism in 1820. During a lecture, he held a compass near a wire carrying an electric current. Oersted noticed that when the compass was close to the wire, the compass needle no longer pointed to the north. This result surprised Oersted because a compass needle is a magnet and only moves from its usual north-south orientation when it is in a magnetic field different from Earth's magnetic field. Oersted tried a few experiments with the compass and the wire and found the results shown in **Figure 13**.

Figure 13 *Oersted's experiments show that an electric current can move a compass needle.*

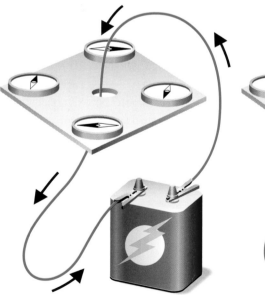

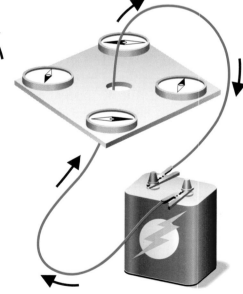

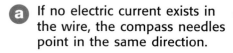

a If no electric current exists in the wire, the compass needles point in the same direction.

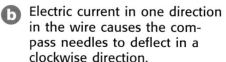

b Electric current in one direction in the wire causes the compass needles to deflect in a clockwise direction.

c Electric current in the opposite direction makes the compass needles deflect in a counterclockwise direction.

More Research From his experiments, Oersted concluded that an electric current produces a magnetic field and that the direction of the magnetic field depends on the direction of the current. The French scientist André-Marie Ampère heard about Oersted's findings and did more research with electricity and magnetism. Together, their work was the first research conducted on electromagnetism. **Electromagnetism** is the interaction between electricity and magnetism.

Compasses Near Magnets

If you try to use a compass near devices that have strong magnets, electromagnets, or electric motors, such as stereo speakers, radios, and televisions, you might notice that the needle of the compass does not always point to the north. Use the results from Oersted's experiments to explain why this occurs. Why do you think it is important for a boater to keep the navigation compass away from the boat's radio?

Using Electromagnetism

Although the magnetic field created by an electric current in a wire may deflect a compass needle, it is not strong enough to be very useful. However, two devices, the solenoid and the electromagnet, strengthen the magnetic field created by a current-carrying wire. Both devices make electromagnetism more useful for practical applications.

Solenoids The scientists mentioned at the beginning of this chapter used a solenoid to levitate a frog. A **solenoid** is a coil of wire that produces a magnetic field when carrying an electric current. A single loop of wire carrying a current does not have a very strong magnetic field. However, if many loops are used to form a coil, the magnetic fields of the individual loops can combine to produce a much stronger magnetic field. In fact, the magnetic field around a solenoid is very similar to the magnetic field of a bar magnet, as shown in
Figure 14. The strength of the magnetic field produced by a solenoid increases as more loops are added and as the current in the wire is increased.

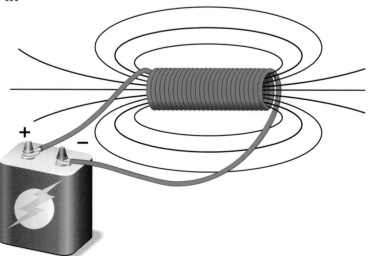

Figure 14 *The ends of the solenoid are like the poles of a magnet.*

Electromagnets

1. Tightly wrap an **insulated copper wire** around a **large iron nail,** leaving 10 cm of wire loose at each end.

2. Remove the insulation from the ends of the wire, and use **electrical tape** to attach the ends against the top and bottom of a **D-cell.**

3. Hold the end of the nail near some **paper clips,** and try to lift them up.

4. While holding the clips up with your electromagnet, remove the wires from the cell.

5. Record your observations in your ScienceLog.

Electromagnets An **electromagnet** is a magnet that consists of a solenoid wrapped around an iron core. The magnetic field produced by the solenoid causes the domains inside the iron core to become better aligned. The magnetic field for the entire electromagnet is the field produced by the solenoid plus the field produced by the magnetized iron core. As a result, the magnetic field produced by an electromagnet may be hundreds of times stronger than the magnetic field produced by just a solenoid with the same number of loops.

The strength of an electromagnet can be made even stronger by increasing the number of loops in the solenoid, by increasing the size of the iron core, and by increasing the electric current in the wire. Some electromagnets are strong enough to lift a car or levitate a train!

Heavy Lifting Do you remember the maglev trains discussed at the beginning of this section? Those trains levitate because there are strong magnets on the cars that are repelled by powerful electromagnets in the rails. Electromagnets are particularly useful because they can be turned on and off as needed. Electromagnets attract objects containing iron only when a current exists in the wire. When there is no current in the wire, the electromagnet is turned off. **Figure 15** shows an example of how this property can be useful.

Figure 15 *The electromagnets used in salvage yards can lift heavy scrap metal when turned on. To put the metal back down, the electromagnet is turned off.*

Self-Check

Can you make an electromagnet by wrapping a coil of wire around a wooden core? Explain your answer.
(See page 120 to check your answer.)

Magnetic Force and Electric Current

At the beginning of this section you learned that an electric current can cause a compass needle to move. The needle, a small magnet, moves because the electric current in a wire creates a magnetic field that exerts a force on the needle. If a current-carrying wire causes a magnet to move, can a magnet cause a current-carrying wire to move? **Figure 16** shows that the answer is yes.

Figure 16 *A magnet exerts a force on a current-carrying wire.*

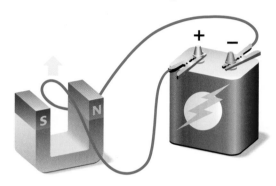

a When a current-carrying wire is placed between two poles of a magnet, the wire will jump up.

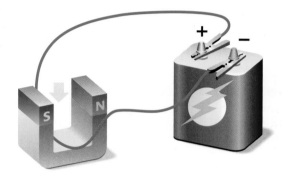

b If the direction of the electric current in the wire is reversed, the wire is pushed down instead of up.

Applications of Electromagnetism

Electromagnetism is useful in your everyday life. You already know that electromagnets can be used to lift heavy objects containing iron. But did you know that you use a solenoid whenever you ring a doorbell or that there are electromagnets in motors? Keep reading to learn how electromagnetism makes these devices work.

Doorbells Many doorbells contain a solenoid with an iron rod inserted part way in it. The electric current in the solenoid is controlled by the doorbell button. When you press the button, a switch in the solenoid circuit closes, creating an electric current in the solenoid. What happens next is shown in **Figure 17.**

Figure 17 *An electric current in the solenoid of a doorbell produces a magnetic field. This field pulls the iron rod through the solenoid, and the rod strikes the bell.*

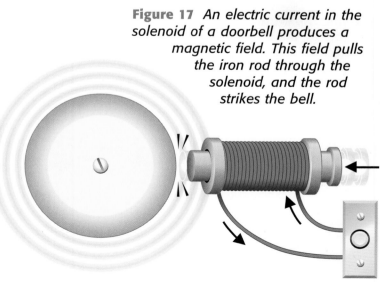

Electric Motors An **electric motor** is a device that changes electrical energy into kinetic energy. All electric motors have an *armature*—a loop or coil of wire that can rotate. The armature is mounted between the poles of a permanent magnet or electromagnet.

In electric motors that use direct current, a device called a *commutator* is attached to the armature to reverse the direction of the electric current in the wire. A commutator is a ring that is split in half and connected to the ends of the armature. Electric current enters the armature through brushes that touch the commutator. Every time the armature and the commutator make a half-turn, the direction of the current is reversed. **Figure 18** shows how a direct-current motor works.

Figure 18 A Direct-Current Electric Motor

Getting Started An electric current in the armature causes the magnet to exert a force on the armature. Because of the direction of the current on either side of the armature, the magnet pulls up on one side and down on the other. This makes the armature rotate.

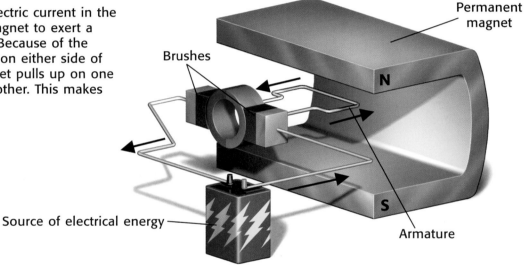

Permanent magnet

Brushes

N

Source of electrical energy

Armature

S

Running the Motor As the armature rotates, the commutator causes the electric current in the coil to change directions. When the electric current is reversed, the side of the coil that was pulled up is pulled down, and the side that was pulled down is pulled up. This keeps the armature rotating.

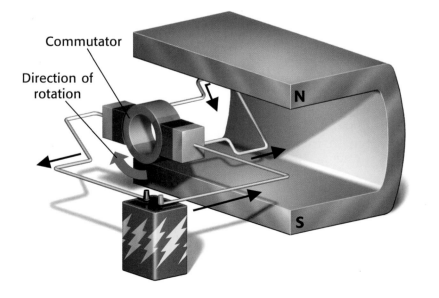

Commutator

Direction of rotation

N

S

Galvanometers A galvanometer is a device used to measure current through the interaction of an electromagnet and a permanent magnet. Galvanometers are sometimes found in equipment used by electricians, such as ammeters and voltmeters. Galvanometers contain an electromagnet placed between the poles of a permanent magnet. The electromagnet is free to rotate and is attached to a pointer. The pointer moves along a scale that shows the size and direction of the current. When there is a current in the coil of the electromagnet, the poles of the electromagnet are repelled by the poles of the permanent magnet. **Figure 19** shows how the parts of a galvanometer work.

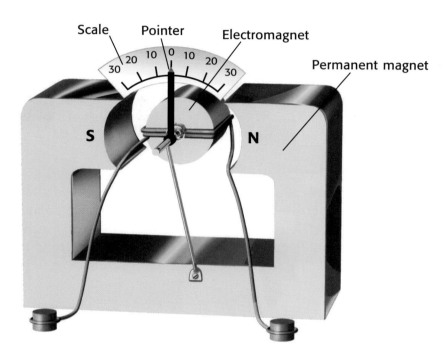

Figure 19 *The pointer will move farther when there is a large current in the electromagnet than when there is a small current.*

SECTION REVIEW

1. Describe what happens when you hold a compass close to a wire carrying a current.

2. How is a solenoid like a bar magnet?

3. What makes the armature in an electric motor rotate?

4. Explain how a solenoid works to make a doorbell ring.

5. **Applying Concepts** What do Hans Christian Oersted's experiments have to do with a galvanometer? Explain your answer.

internet**connect**

SC*L*INKS.
NSTA

TOPIC: Electromagnetism
GO TO: www.scilinks.org
*sci***LINKS NUMBER:** HSTP440

Terms to Learn

electromagnetic induction
generator
transformer

What You'll Do

◆ Explain how a magnetic field can produce an electric current.
◆ Explain how electromagnetic induction is used in a generator.
◆ Compare step-up and step-down transformers.

Electricity from Magnetism

When you use an electric appliance or turn on a light in your home, you probably don't think about where the electrical energy comes from. For most people, an electric power company supplies their home with electrical energy. In this section, you'll learn how a magnetic field can produce an electric current and how power companies use this process to supply electrical energy.

Electric Current from a Magnetic Field

After Oersted discovered that an electric current could produce a magnetic field, scientists began to wonder if a magnetic field could produce an electric current. In 1831, two scientists—Michael Faraday, from Great Britain, and Joseph Henry, from the United States—independently solved this problem. Although Henry was the first to make the discovery, Faraday's results are better known because Faraday published his results first and reported them in greater detail.

Faraday's Failure? In his experiments, Faraday used a setup similar to the one shown in **Figure 20.** Faraday hoped that the magnetic field created by the electromagnet would create—or induce—an electric current in the second wire. But no matter how strong the electromagnet was, no electric current could be produced in the second wire.

Figure 20 Faraday's Setup

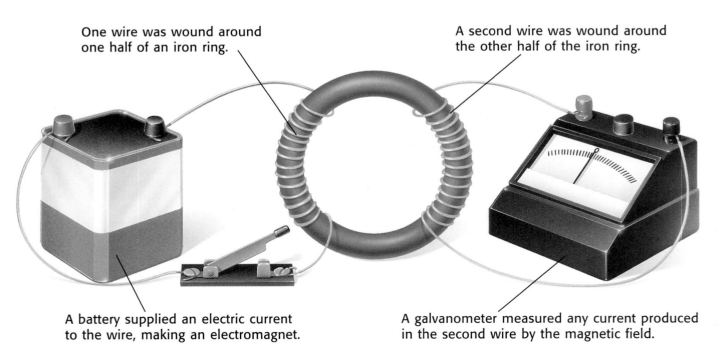

One wire was wound around one half of an iron ring.

A second wire was wound around the other half of the iron ring.

A battery supplied an electric current to the wire, making an electromagnet.

A galvanometer measured any current produced in the second wire by the magnetic field.

Success for an Instant As Faraday experimented with this electromagnetic ring, he noticed something interesting. At the instant he connected the wires of the electromagnet to the battery, the galvanometer pointer moved, indicating that an electric current was present. The pointer moved again at the instant he disconnected the electromagnet. But as long as the electromagnet was fully connected to the battery, the galvanometer measured no electric current.

Faraday realized that electric current in the second wire was produced only when the magnetic field was changing—in this case, when the magnetic field was turned on and off as the battery was connected and disconnected. The process by which an electric current is produced by a changing magnetic field is called **electromagnetic induction.** Faraday did many more experiments on electromagnetic induction. Some of his results are summarized in **Figure 21.**

Figure 21 *The size and direction of the electric current induced by a changing magnetic field depends on several factors.*

a An electric current is induced when you move a magnet through a coil of wire.

b A greater electric current is induced if you move the magnet faster through the coil because the magnetic field is changing faster.

c A greater electric current is induced if you add more loops of wire. This magnet is moving at the same speed as the magnet in (b).

d The induced electric current reverses direction if the magnet is pulled out rather than pushed in.

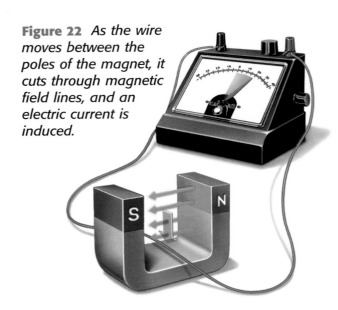

Figure 22 *As the wire moves between the poles of the magnet, it cuts through magnetic field lines, and an electric current is induced.*

Inducing Electric Current Faraday's experiments also showed that the magnetic field around a wire can be changed by moving either the magnet or the wire. Therefore, an electric current could be induced by moving a magnet in a coil of wire or by moving a wire between the poles of a magnet.

One way to remember when an electric current is produced by electromagnetic induction is to consider the magnetic field lines between the poles of the magnet. An electric current is induced only when a wire cuts through, or crosses, the magnetic field lines, as shown in **Figure 22.** This is because the magnetic force causes electric charges to move through the wire as the wire moves through the magnetic field.

Applications of Electromagnetic Induction

Electromagnetic induction is very important for the production of electrical energy at an electric power plant, and it is important for the transmission of energy from the plant to your home. Generators and transformers work on the principle of electromagnetic induction and are used by power plants to provide the electrical energy that you need every day.

Generators A **generator** is a device that uses electromagnetic induction to convert kinetic energy into electrical energy. **Figure 23** shows the parts of a simple generator, and **Figure 24,** on the next page, explains how the generator works.

Figure 23
Parts of a Simple Generator

Generators contain a **coil of wire** attached to a rod that is free to rotate. This generator has a crank that is used to turn the coil.

Slip rings are attached to the ends of the wire in the coil.

Electric current leaves the generator when the slip rings touch a pair of **brushes.**

The coil is placed between the poles of a **permanent magnet** or electromagnet.

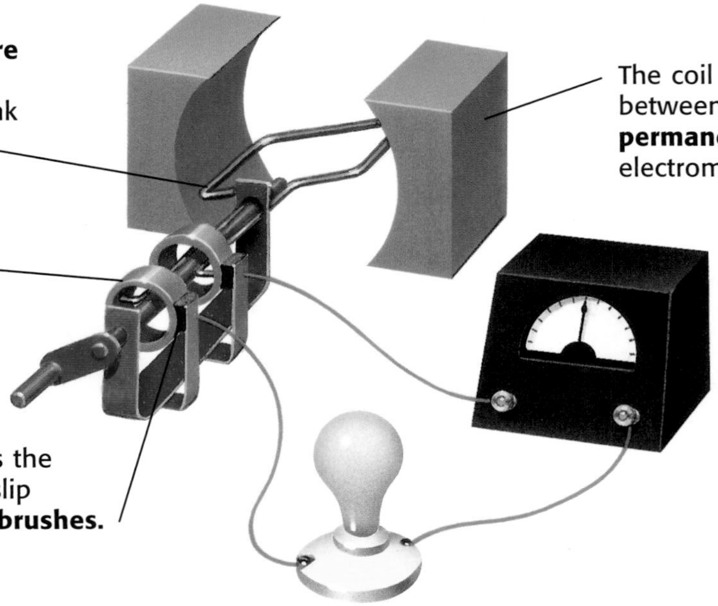

Figure 24 How a Generator Works

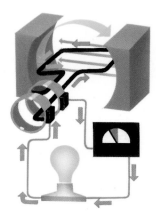

1 As the crank is turned, the rotating coil cuts through the magnetic field lines of the magnet, and an electric current is induced in the wire.

2 When the coil is not cutting through the magnetic field lines, no electric current is induced.

3 As the coil continues to rotate, the magnetic field lines are cut from a different direction, and an electric current is induced in the opposite direction.

Alternating Current The electric current produced by the generator shown in Figure 24 changes direction each time the coil makes a half-turn. Because the electric current continually changes direction, the electric current is an alternating current. Generators in power plants also produce alternating current. But generators in power plants are much larger and contain many coils of wire instead of just one. In most large generators, the magnet is turned instead of the coils.

Generating Electrical Energy The energy that generators convert to electrical energy comes from different sources. In nuclear power plants, thermal energy from a nuclear reaction boils water to produce steam, which turns a turbine. The turbine turns the magnet of the generator, inducing an electric current and generating electrical energy. **Figure 25** shows a similar process in a hydroelectric power plant.

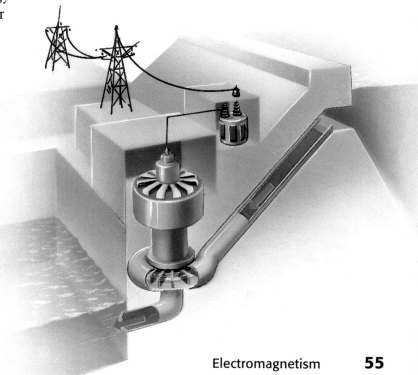

Figure 25 *As water flows down a chute, it turns a turbine. The turbine spins the magnet of the generator, inducing an electric current.*

Transformers Another device that relies on electromagnetic induction is a transformer. A **transformer** increases or decreases the voltage of an alternating current. A simple transformer consists of two coils of wire wrapped around an iron ring.

Alternating current from an electrical energy source is supplied to one coil, called the primary coil. The electric current makes the ring an electromagnet. But the electric current in the primary coil is alternating, so the magnetic field of the electromagnet changes with every change in electric current direction. The changing magnetic field in the iron ring induces an electric current in the other coil, called the secondary coil.

Step-Up, Step-Down The number of loops in the primary and secondary coils of a transformer determines whether it increases or decreases the voltage. If a transformer increases voltage, it is a step-up transformer. If a transformer decreases voltage, it is a step-down transformer. Both kinds of transformers are shown in **Figure 26.**

Figure 26 *Transformers can either increase or decrease voltage.*

The primary coil of a **step-up transformer** has fewer loops than the secondary coil. So the voltage of the electric current in the secondary coil is higher than the voltage of the electric current in the primary coil. Therefore, voltage is increased.

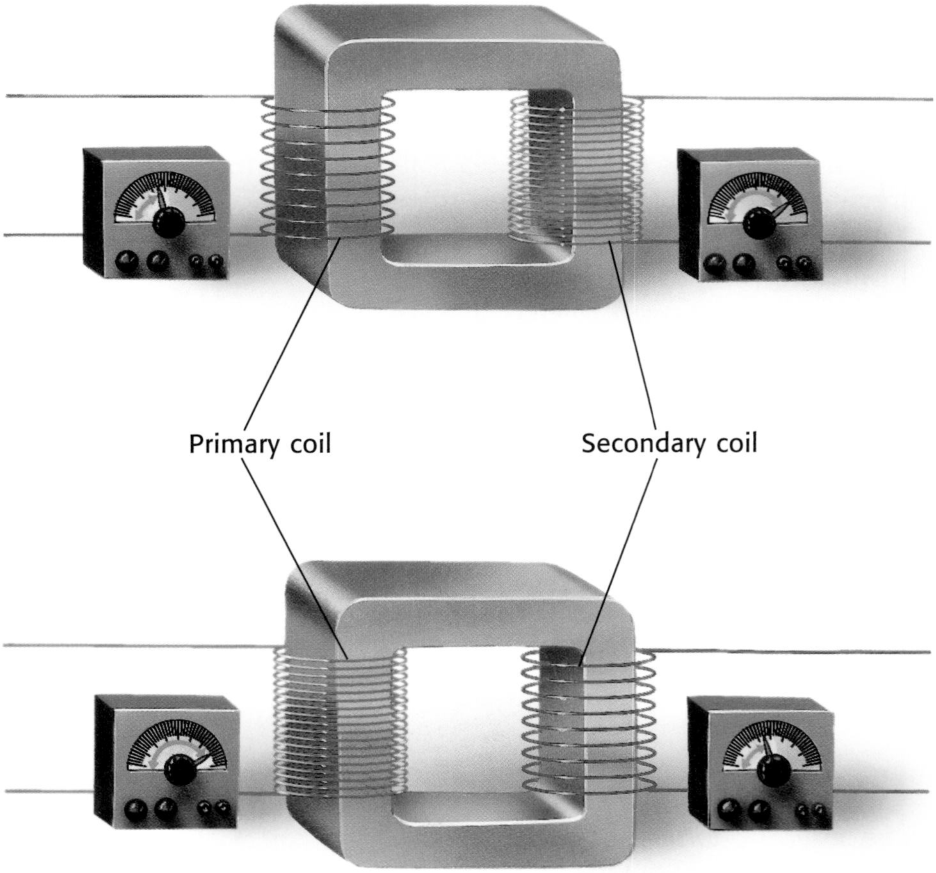

Primary coil   Secondary coil

The primary coil of a **step-down transformer** has more loops than the secondary coil. So the voltage of the electric current in the secondary coil is lower than the voltage of the electric current in the primary coil. Therefore, voltage is decreased.

Electrical Energy for Your Home The electric current that provides your home with electrical energy is usually transformed three times before it reaches your home. Generators at the power plants produce electric current with high voltage. To decrease the loss of power that occurs during transmission over long distance, the voltage is increased thousands of times with a step-up transformer. Of course, the voltage must be decreased before it is distributed to households. Two different step-down transformers are used before the electric current reaches consumers. **Figure 27** shows how electric current is transformed on its way to your home.

Figure 27 *Electric current is transformed three times before reaching your home.*

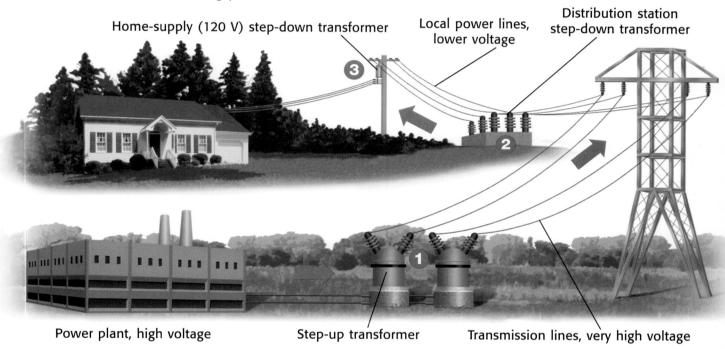

Home-supply (120 V) step-down transformer

Local power lines, lower voltage

Distribution station step-down transformer

Power plant, high voltage

Step-up transformer

Transmission lines, very high voltage

SECTION REVIEW

1. How does a generator produce an electric current?

2. Explain why rotating either the coil or the magnet induces an electric current in a generator.

3. **Inferring Conclusions** One reason why electric power plants do not distribute electrical energy as direct current is that direct current cannot be transformed. Explain why not.

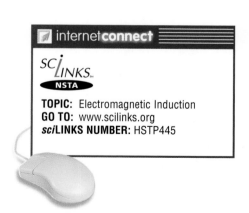

internet**connect**

SC*i*LINKS

NSTA

TOPIC: Electromagnetic Induction
GO TO: www.scilinks.org
*sci*LINKS NUMBER: HSTP445

Skill Builder Lab

Magnetic Mystery

Every magnet is surrounded by a magnetic field. Magnetic field lines show the shape of the magnetic field. These lines can be modeled by using iron filings. The iron filings are affected by the magnetic field, and they fall into lines showing the field. In this lab, you will first learn about magnetic fields, and then you will use this knowledge to identify a mystery magnet's shape and orientation based on observations of the field lines.

MATERIALS

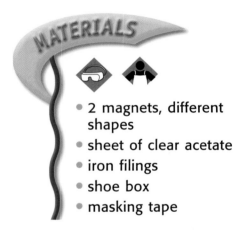

- 2 magnets, different shapes
- sheet of clear acetate
- iron filings
- shoe box
- masking tape

Collect Data

1 Lay one of the magnets flat on a table.

2 Place a sheet of clear acetate over the magnet. Sprinkle some iron filings on the acetate. In your ScienceLog, draw the magnet and the magnetic field lines. Remove the acetate, and pour the iron filings back into the container.

3 Place your magnet so that one end is pointing up. Repeat step 2.

4 Place your magnet on its side. Repeat step 2.

5 Repeat steps 1 through 4 with the other magnet.

Conduct an Experiment

6 Create a magnetic mystery for another team. Remove the lid from a shoe box. Tape a magnet under the lid. Orient the magnet so that determining the shape of the magnetic field and the orientation of the magnet will be challenging. Once the magnet is secure, place the lid on the box.

7 Exchange boxes with another team.

8 Without opening the box, use the sheet of acetate and the iron filings to determine the shape of the magnetic field of the magnet in the box. Make a drawing of the magnetic field lines.

Draw Conclusions

9 Identify the shape and orientation of the magnet in your magnetic mystery box. Draw a picture of your conclusion.

Electricity from Magnetism

You use electricity every day. But did you ever wonder where it comes from? Some of the electrical energy you use is converted from chemical energy in cells or batteries. But what about when you plug a lamp into a wall outlet? In this lab, you will see how electricity can be generated from magnetism.

MATERIALS

- sandpaper
- 150 cm of magnet wire
- cardboard tube
- commercial galvanometer
- 2 insulated wires with alligator clips, each approximately 30 cm long
- strong bar magnet

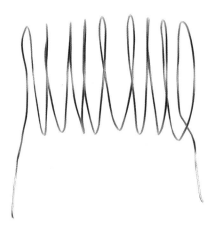

Form a Hypothesis

1 How can electricity be generated from magnetism? Write a statement to answer the question.

Test the Hypothesis

2 Sand the enamel from the last 3 cm of each end of the magnet wire. Wrap the wire around the tube to make a coil. Attach the ends of the wire to the galvanometer, using the insulated wires.

3 While watching the galvanometer, move a bar magnet into the coil, hold it there for a moment, and then remove it. Record your observations.

4 Repeat step 3 several times, moving the magnet at different speeds.

5 Hold the magnet still, and pass the coil over the magnet. Record your observations.

Analyze the Results

6 How does the speed of the magnet affect the size of the electric current?

7 How is the direction of the electric current affected by the motion of the magnet?

Draw Conclusions

8 Would an electric current still be generated if the wire were broken? Why or why not?

9 Could a stationary magnet be used to generate an electric current? Explain.

Chapter Highlights

Vocabulary

magnet *(p. 38)*
poles *(p. 38)*
magnetic force *(p. 39)*

Section Notes

- All magnets have two poles. One pole will always point to the north if allowed to rotate freely, and it is called the north pole. The other pole is called the south pole.

- Like magnetic poles repel each other; opposite magnetic poles attract.

- All magnets are surrounded by a magnetic field. The shape of that magnetic field can be shown with magnetic field lines.

- A material is magnetic if its domains are aligned. Iron, nickel, and cobalt atoms group together in domains.

- Magnets can be classified as ferromagnets, electromagnets, temporary magnets, and permanent magnets. A magnet can belong to more than one group.

- Earth acts as if it has a big bar magnet in its core.

- Compass needles and the north pole of magnets point to Earth's magnetic south pole—which is close to Earth's geographic North Pole.

- Auroras are most commonly seen near Earth's magnetic poles because Earth's magnetic fields bend inward at the poles.

Vocabulary

electromagnetism *(p. 47)*
solenoid *(p. 47)*
electromagnet *(p. 48)*
electric motor *(p. 50)*

Section Notes

- Oersted discovered that a wire carrying an electric current produces a magnetic field.

- Electromagnetism is the interaction between electricity and magnetism.

- A solenoid is a coil of current-carrying wire that produces a magnetic field.

- An electromagnet is a solenoid with an iron core. The electromagnet has a stronger magnetic field than a solenoid of the same size does.

- Increasing the current in a solenoid or an electromagnet increases the magnetic field.

☑ Skills Check

Visual Understanding

ELECTROMAGNETISM The two important concepts in electromagnetism were discovered by Oersted and Faraday. Figure 13 on page 46 summarizes Oersted's work, which showed that an electric current can produce a magnetic field.

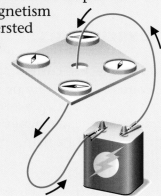

ELECTROMAGNETIC INDUCTION Faraday's work showed that a changing magnetic field can induce an electric current in a wire. His results are summarized in Figure 21 on page 53.

- Increasing the number of loops on a solenoid or an electromagnet increases the magnetic field.

- A magnet can exert a force on a wire carrying a current.

- In a doorbell, the magnetic field of a solenoid pulls an iron rod, and the iron rod strikes the bell.

- The magnetic force between a magnet and wires carrying an electric current makes an electric motor turn.

- An electric motor converts electrical energy into kinetic energy.

- A galvanometer measures current by using the magnetic force between an electromagnet and a permanent magnet.

Labs

Build a DC Motor (p. 98)

Vocabulary

electromagnetic induction (p. 53)
generator (p. 54)
transformer (p. 56)

Section Notes

- Faraday discovered that a changing magnetic field can create an electric current in a wire. This is called electromagnetic induction.

- Generators use electromagnetic induction to convert kinetic energy into electrical energy.

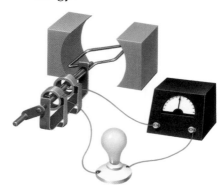

- Kinetic energy can be supplied to a generator in different ways.

- Transformers increase or decrease the voltage of an alternating current using electromagnetic induction.

- A step-up transformer increases the voltage of an alternating current. Its primary coil has fewer loops than its secondary coil.

- A step-down transformer decreases the voltage of an alternating current. Its primary coil has more loops than its secondary coil.

Chapter Review

USING VOCABULARY

To complete the following sentences, choose the correct term from each pair of terms listed below:

1. All magnets have two __?__. *(magnetic forces* or *poles)*

2. A(n) __?__ converts kinetic energy into electrical energy. *(electric motor* or *generator)*

3. __?__ occurs when an electric current is produced by a changing magnetic field. *(Electromagnetic induction* or *Magnetic force)*

4. The interaction between electricity and magnetism is called __?__. *(electromagnetism* or *electromagnetic induction)*

UNDERSTANDING CONCEPTS

Multiple Choice

5. The region around a magnet in which magnetic forces can act is called the
   a. magnetic field.　　c. pole.
   b. domain.　　　　　d. solenoid.

6. An electric fan has an electric motor inside to change
   a. kinetic energy into electrical energy.
   b. thermal energy into electrical energy.
   c. electrical energy into thermal energy.
   d. electrical energy into kinetic energy.

7. The marked end of a compass needle always points directly to
   a. Earth's geographic South Pole.
   b. Earth's geographic North Pole.
   c. a magnet's south pole.
   d. a magnet's north pole.

8. A device that increases the voltage of an alternating current is called a(n)
   a. electric motor.
   b. galvanometer.
   c. step-up transformer.
   d. step-down transformer.

9. The magnetic field of a solenoid can be increased by
   a. adding more loops.
   b. increasing the current.
   c. putting an iron core inside the coil to make an electromagnet.
   d. All of the above

10. What do you end up with if you cut a magnet in half?
    a. one north-pole piece and one south-pole piece
    b. two unmagnetized pieces
    c. two pieces, each with a north pole and a south pole
    d. two north-pole pieces

Short Answer

11. Explain why auroras are seen mostly near the North and South Poles.

12. Compare the function of a generator with the function of an electric motor.

13. Explain why some pieces of iron are more magnetic than others.

Concept Mapping

14. Use the following terms to create a concept map: electromagnetism, electricity, magnetism, electromagnetic induction, generator, transformer.

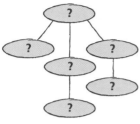

15. You win a hand-powered flashlight as a prize in your school science fair. The flashlight has a clear plastic case so you can look inside to see how it works. When you press the handle, a gray ring spins between two coils of wire. The ends of the wire are connected to the light bulb. So when you press the handle, the light bulb glows. Explain how an electric current is produced to light the bulb. (Hint: Paper clips are attracted to the gray ring.)

16. Fire doors are doors that can slow the spread of fire from room to room when they are closed. In some buildings, fire doors are held open by electromagnets. The electromagnets are controlled by the building's fire alarm system. If a fire is detected, the doors automatically shut. Explain why electromagnets are used instead of permanent magnets.

17. Study the solenoids and electromagnets shown below. Rank them in order of strongest magnetic field to weakest magnetic field. Explain your ranking.

a

Current = 2 A

b

Current = 2 A

c

Current = 4 A

d

Current = 4 A

Reading Check-up

Take a minute to review your answers to the Pre-Reading Questions found at the bottom of page 36. Have your answers changed? If necessary, revise your answers based on what you have learned since you began this chapter.

Geomagnetic Storms

On March 13, 1989, a storm hit Montreal, Quebec. But this wasn't an ordinary storm. This was a geomagnetic storm that caused an electrical blackout. About 6 million people went without electricity for 9 hours.

What Is a Geomagnetic Storm?

To understand a geomagnetic storm, you must first know a few things about the sun. By looking closely at the surface of the sun, scientists have discovered that it has cycles of very violent activity. Powerful eruptions called solar flares occur periodically, sending charged particles outward at almost the speed of light and with the energy of millions of hydrogen bombs. As particles explode away from the solar surface, they create a solar wind of charged particles that travels several million kilometers per hour through space between the sun and the Earth. A geomagnetic storm occurs when the solar wind sweeps across Earth's atmosphere, causing a variety of disturbances.

Grids and Pipelines

Geomagnetic storms happen frequently, especially in the north. As the people of Quebec found out in 1989, such storms can interfere with systems used to operate power grids. They can also cause heavy static in long-distance radio reception and can affect the orbit of satellites. Geomagnetic storms can even cause corrosion in the metal of petroleum pipelines. In fact, scientists are not sure that they know of all the systems and materials that are affected by geomagnetic storms.

Knowledge Is the First Line of Defense

Solar flares are not well understood and are difficult to predict. There may be nothing that can be done to stop geomagnetic storms, but understanding them better is the first step toward protecting valuable systems from an eruption's effects. Scientists prepared several satellites to study the sun's activity and solar flares in 2000 and 2001. By studying solar eruptions, scientists think they can predict a geomagnetic storm 50 to 70 hours in advance. This could give industries affected by these storms time to protect their systems.

Solar Sails for Solar Wind

▶ Do research on solar flares and geomagnetic storms. Government agencies and universities have a number of programs, including satellites, to study and predict solar events. Create a model or a poster to explain something you learned from your research.

◀ *Solar flares on the sun can result in geomagnetic storms here on Earth.*

Magnets in Medicine

Think about what it would be like to peer inside the human body to locate a tumor, find tiny blockages in blood vessels, or even identify damage to the brain. Medical technology known as magnetic resonance imaging (MRI) gives doctors a quick and painless way to see and diagnose these problems and more.

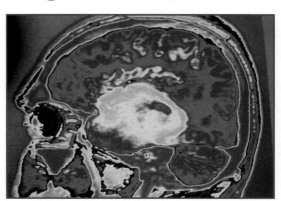

▲ *This color-enhanced MRI image of a brain shows a tumor (tinted yellow). The tumor was removed, and the patient resumed a healthy life.*

Magnetic Images

Like X rays, MRI creates pictures of a person's internal organs and skeleton. But MRI produces clearer pictures than X rays do, and MRI does not expose the body to the potentially harmful radiation of X rays. Instead, MRI uses powerful electromagnets and radio waves to create images.

The patient is placed in a large machine. An electric current in the electromagnet creates a powerful magnetic field around the patient. Because the human body is composed mostly of fat and water, there are many hydrogen atoms in the body. The magnetic field causes the nuclei of the hydrogen atoms to align in the direction of the magnetic field. Then another, weaker magnetic signal is sent out to the cells. The energy in this signal causes some hydrogen nuclei to change their position. As the signal's energy is absorbed and then released by the hydrogen nuclei, the MRI machine collects the signals and its computer converts the information into an image.

A Diagnostic Device

MRI is particularly useful for locating small tumors, revealing subtle changes in the brain, pinpointing blockages in blood vessels, and showing damage to the spinal cord. This technology also allows doctors to observe the function of specific body parts, such as the ears, heart, muscles, tendons, and blood vessels.

Researchers are experimenting with more-powerful magnets that work on other types of atoms. This technology is known as magnetic resonance spectroscopy (MRS). One current use of MRS is to monitor the effectiveness of chemotherapy in cancer patients. Doctors analyze MRS images to find chemical changes that might indicate whether the therapy is successful.

Picture This

▶ You may be familiar with X rays, but procedures like CAT or CT scans and MRI may be new to you. Research the different imaging tools—including X-ray tomography, CT or CAT scans, and MRI—that doctors can use to diagnose and treat injuries and disease. Select one of the imaging processes and make a model of how it works to demonstrate to the class. Be sure to include the procedure's advantages and disadvantages and the types of injuries or diseases for which it is used.

Electronic Technology

Pre-Reading
Questions

1. What is an electronic
   device?

2. What are some electronic
   devices used for communication?

3. What are the parts of a
   computer?

ELECTRONIC TRAFFIC CONTROL

Is this a photo of a futuristic town, seen from high in the
air? Look more closely. Those pathways are not streets and
highways. They are tiny, complex electrical pathways on a
microchip, a device that controls the flow of electric current. Microchips are the basic building blocks of computers
and other high-tech devices. In this chapter, you will learn
how electronic devices, such as computers, radios, and
televisions, work and how circuit boards are made and
electronic signals are produced.

TALKING LONG DISTANCE

Using a telephone allows you to communicate with someone from a distance. In this activity, you'll construct a model of a telephone.

Procedure

1. Thread one end of a **piece of string** through the hole in the bottom of one **empty coffee can.**

2. Tie a knot in the end of the string inside the can. The knot should be large enough to keep the string in place. The rest of the string should be coming out of the bottom of the can.

3. Repeat steps 1 and 2 with **another can** and the other end of the string.

4. Hold one can and have a classmate hold the other. Walk away from each other until the string is pulled fairly taut.

5. Speak into your can while your classmate holds the other can at his or her ear. Switch roles.

Analysis

6. In your ScienceLog, describe what you heard.

7. How is your apparatus similar to a real telephone? How is it different?

8. How are signals sent back and forth along the string?

9. Why do you think it was important to pull the string taut?

Terms to Learn

circuit board   diode
semiconductor   transistor
doping   integrated circuit

What You'll Do

◆ Describe semiconductors and how their conductivity can be modified.
◆ Identify diodes, transistors, and integrated circuits as electronic components.
◆ Explain how integrated circuits have influenced electronic technology.
◆ Compare vacuum tubes and transistors.

Electronic Components

Electronic devices rely on electrical energy, but not in the same way that appliances and machines do. Some machines can convert electrical energy into light, thermal, and mechanical energy in order to do work. Electronic devices use electrical energy to transmit information.

Inside an Electronic Device

A TV remote control is an example of an electronic device. It transmits information to a TV about volume levels and what channel to display. Have you ever looked inside of a TV remote control? If so, you would have seen something similar to **Figure 1.** A remote control contains a **circuit board,** a collection of hundreds of tiny circuits that supply electric current to the various parts of an electronic device.

To change channels or adjust the volume on the TV, you push buttons on the remote control. When you push a button, a tiny bulb called a light-emitting diode (DIE OHD), or LED, sends information to the TV in the form of infrared light. The components of the circuit board you see in Figure 1 control the electric current within the remote control in order to send the correct information to the TV. In this section you'll learn about some components of electronic devices and how they control electric current.

Figure 1 *Each part of a remote control has a role in transmitting information.*

Semiconductors

Many electronic components are made from semiconductors (SEM i kuhn DUHK tuhrz). A **semiconductor** is a substance that conducts an electric current better than an insulator but not as well as a conductor. The use of semiconductors has resulted in some incredible advances in electronic technology.

How Do Semiconductors Work? The way a semiconductor conducts electric current is based on how its electrons are arranged. Silicon (Si) is a widely used semiconductor in electronic technology. When silicon atoms bond, they share their valence electrons, as shown in **Figure 2.** Because all the valence electrons are shared, there are no electrons free to create much electric current in the semiconductor. So why are semiconductors like silicon used in electronic devices? Because their conductivity can be modified.

Doping In order to modify the conductivity of a semiconductor, its arrangement of electrons must be altered. This is done through **doping** (DOHP eeng), the process of replacing a few atoms of a semiconductor with a few atoms of another substance that have a different number of valence electrons. Two types of doped semiconductors are shown in **Figure 3.**

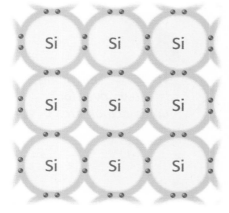

Figure 2 *Each silicon atom shares its four valence electrons with other silicon atoms.*

Figure 3 Types of Doped Semiconductors

N-type semiconductor An atom of arsenic (As) has five electrons in its outermost energy level. Replacing a silicon atom with an arsenic atom results in an "extra" electron.

P-type semiconductor An atom of gallium (Ga) has three electrons in its outermost energy level. Replacing a silicon atom with a gallium atom results in a "hole" where an electron could be.

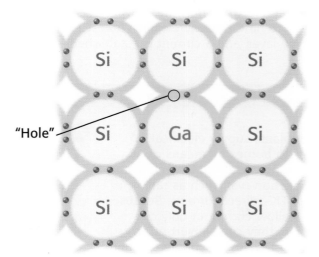

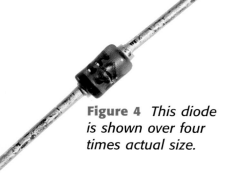

Figure 4 *This diode is shown over four times actual size.*

Diodes

Layers of semiconductors can be put together like sandwiches to make electronic components. For example, joining one layer of an n-type semiconductor and one layer of a p-type semiconductor creates a semiconductor diode, like the one shown in **Figure 4**. A **diode** is an electronic component that allows electric current in only one direction.

Diodes in Circuits The way in which a diode works has to do with its semiconductor layers. Where the p-type and n-type layers meet, some "extra" electrons move from the n-type layer to fill some "holes" in the p-type layer. This gives the p-type layer a negative charge and the n-type layer a positive charge. If a diode is connected to a source of electrical energy so that the positive terminal is closest to the p-type layer, a current is established. However, if the terminals are reversed so that the negative terminal is closest to the p-type layer, there will be no current. **Figure 5** illustrates how a diode works.

Figure 5 **How a Diode Works**

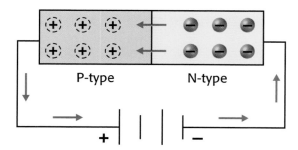

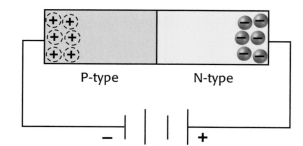

a Electrons move from the negatively charged p-type layer toward the positive terminal. As a result, electrons from the n-type layer can move to fill the newly created "holes" in the p-type layer, and a current is established.

b Electrons in the negatively charged p-type layer are repelled by the negative terminal. No new "holes" are created, so no electrons can move from the n-type layer to the p-type layer. As a result, there is no current.

Using Diodes to Change AC to DC

Power plants supply electrical energy to homes by means of AC (alternating current). Many electronic systems, however, such as radios, require DC (direct current). Because diodes allow current in only one direction, they can convert AC to pulses of DC. An AC adapter contains a diode.

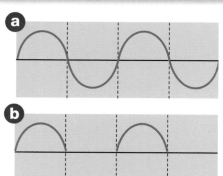

a Alternating current, which periodically changes direction, is supplied to the diode.

b The diode blocks the current in one direction, resulting in pulsed direct current.

Transistors

What do you get when you sandwich three layers of semi-conductors together? A transistor! A **transistor** is an electronic component that can be used as an amplifier or as a switch. Transistors, such as the one shown in **Figure 6,** can be NPN or PNP transistors. An NPN transistor consists of one layer of a p-type semiconductor between two layers of an n-type semi-conductor. A PNP transistor consists of one layer of an n-type semiconductor between two layers of a p-type semiconductor. When connected in a circuit, the transistor's "legs" conduct electric current into and out of the transistor's layers.

Figure 6 *This transistor is smaller than a pencil eraser!*

Transistors as Amplifiers To see how a transistor is used as an amplifier, look at the circuit shown in **Figure 7.** A microphone does not supply a large enough current to operate a loudspeaker. But if a transistor is used, the small electric current in the microphone side of the circuit can trigger a larger electric current in the loudspeaker side of the circuit. The electric current can be larger because of the large source of electrical energy in the loudspeaker side of the circuit.

Figure 7 A Transistor as an Amplifier

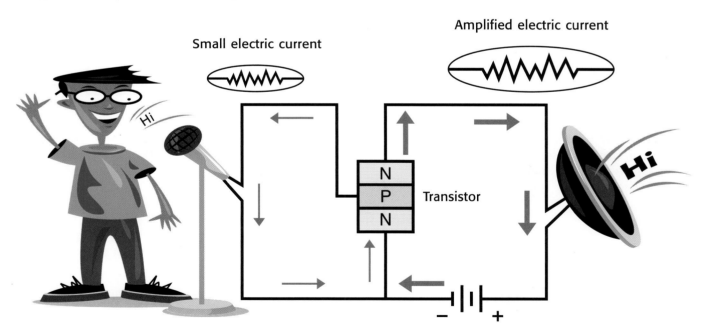

1 Sound waves from your voice enter the microphone. As a result, a small electric current is produced in the micro-phone side of the circuit.

2 A transistor allows the small electric current to trigger a larger electric current that operates the loudspeaker.

3 The current in the loud-speaker is identical to the current produced by the microphone, except that it has a larger amplitude.

Transistors as Switches A transistor can also be used as an electronic on-off switch in a circuit. When the manual switch in **Figure 8** is closed, a small current is established in the left side of the circuit. The small current causes the transistor to close the right side of the circuit. As a result, a larger current, which operates a small motor, is established in the right side of the circuit. Basically, you switch on a small current, and the transistor switches on a larger current. If the manual switch is opened, there will no longer be a current in the left side of the circuit. As a result, the transistor will switch off the current that operates the motor. Circuits similar to the one in Figure 8 can be found in remote-controlled toy cars and in windshield wipers.

Figure 8 A Transistor as a Switch

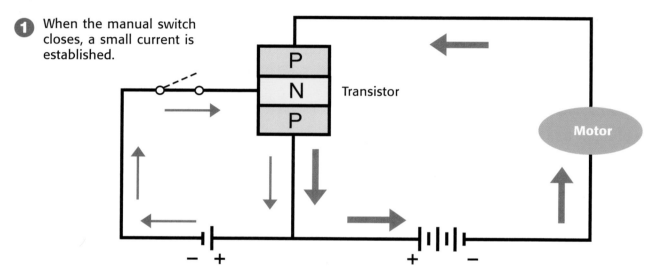

1 When the manual switch closes, a small current is established.

Transistor

Motor

2 The transistor acts as a switch because a small current in the transistor closes the right side of the circuit. A larger current can therefore operate the motor.

Integrated Circuits Look at the electronic device shown in **Figure 9.** This is an **integrated** (IN tuh GRAYT ed) **circuit,** an entire circuit containing many transistors and other electronic components formed on a single silicon chip. The components of the circuit are constructed on the silicon layer by doping the silicon at specific places.

Integrated circuits and circuit boards, such as the one in the TV remote control at the beginning of this section, have helped shrink electronic systems. Because several complete circuits can fit into one integrated circuit, complicated electronic systems can be made very small. In addition, integrated circuit devices can operate at high speeds because the electric charges traveling through them do not have to travel very far.

Figure 9 *This integrated circuit contains thousands of electronic components, yet its dimensions are only about 1 × 3 cm!*

Electronic Technology of Yesterday . . .

Before the invention of transistors and semiconductor diodes, electronic devices used vacuum tubes, like the one shown here. Vacuum tubes can amplify electric current and convert AC to DC. However, vacuum tubes are much larger, give off more thermal energy, and don't last as long as transistors and semiconductor diodes. Early radios were very bulky because they were made with vacuum tubes. Another reason the radios had to be so big was so that the vacuum tubes had space to give off thermal energy.

. . . and Today

Modern radios are built with transistors and semiconductor diodes. Frequently, a radio comes with other features, such as a clock or a tape deck, all packaged in less space than a radio made with vacuum tubes. Modern electronic components have enabled electronic devices to become much smaller and perform more functions.

SECTION REVIEW

1. Describe how p-type and n-type semiconductors are made.

2. Explain how a diode changes AC to DC.

3. What two purposes do transistors serve?

4. **Comparing Concepts** How might an electronic system that uses vacuum tubes be different from one that uses integrated circuits?

internet**connect**

SC*i*LINKS.
NSTA

TOPIC: Transistors
GO TO: www.scilinks.org
*sci*LINKS NUMBER: HSTP455

Terms to Learn

telecommunication
signal
analog signal
digital signal

What You'll Do

◆ Describe how signals transmit information.
◆ Explain how a telephone works.
◆ Compare analog and digital signals.
◆ Describe how radios and televisions transmit information.

Communication Technology

One of the first electronic communication devices was the telegraph, which was invented in the 1830s. **Figure 10** shows the telegraph key invented by Samuel Morse. The telegraph used an electric current to send messages between two devices connected by wires. Telegraph operators sent messages in Morse code by tapping the telegraph key to close an electric circuit, causing "clicks" at the receiving end of the telegraph. Although telegraphs are not used much today, they served as the first example of **telecommunication,** the sending of information across long distances by electronic means. In this section you'll learn about some electronic devices that are used for communication.

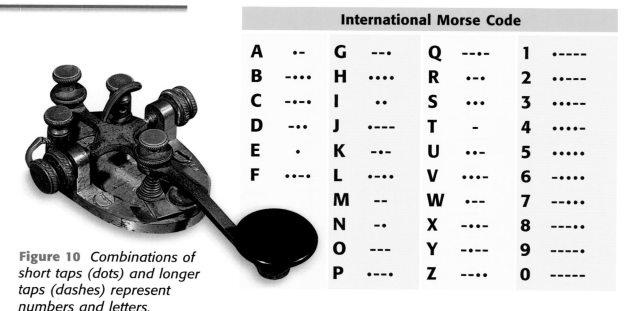

International Morse Code							
A	·‒	G	‒‒·	Q	‒‒·‒	1	·‒‒‒‒
B	‒···	H	····	R	·‒·	2	··‒‒‒
C	‒·‒·	I	··	S	···	3	···‒‒
D	‒··	J	·‒‒‒	T	‒	4	····‒
E	·	K	‒·‒	U	··‒	5	·····
F	··‒·	L	·‒··	V	···‒	6	‒····
		M	‒‒	W	·‒‒	7	‒‒···
		N	‒·	X	‒··‒	8	‒‒‒··
		O	‒‒‒	Y	‒·‒‒	9	‒‒‒‒·
		P	·‒‒·	Z	‒‒··	0	‒‒‒‒‒

Figure 10 *Combinations of short taps (dots) and longer taps (dashes) represent numbers and letters.*

Activity

Write out a message to a friend using Morse code.

···· · ‒··· ·‒·· ‒‒‒
H E L L O

Try at Home

Communicating with Signals

Electronic communication devices transmit information by using signals. A **signal** is something that represents information. A signal can be a command, a sound, or a series of numbers and letters. Often a signal travels better when contained in another form of energy, called a *carrier.* For example, in a telegraph, electric current is the carrier of the signals created by tapping the telegraph key. Two types of signals that carry information in electronic communication devices are analog signals and digital signals.

Analog Signals

The signals that carry the information through telephone lines are analog signals. An **analog** (AN uh LAHG) **signal** is a signal whose properties, such as amplitude and frequency, can change continuously according to changes in the original information. For example, when you talk on the phone, the sound of your voice is converted into changing electric current in the form of a wave. This wave is an analog signal that is similar in frequency and amplitude to the original sound wave. Just remember that the analog signal is not a sound wave—it is a wave of electric current.

Talking on the Phone Look at the telephone in **Figure 11.** The part you talk into is called the transmitter, and the part you listen to is called the receiver. The transmitter converts the sound waves produced when you speak into the analog signal that travels through phone wires to the receiver of another phone. The receiver converts the analog signal back into the sound of your voice.

Geology
CONNECTION

A seismograph is a device geologists use to record earthquakes. A seismograph produces a seismogram—wavy lines on paper that represent earthquake waves. A seismogram is an example of an analog signal. The waves on a seismogram are similar in amplitude and frequency to the waves produced by an earthquake. As the earthquake changes in magnitude, the lines change accordingly.

Figure 11 How a Telephone Works

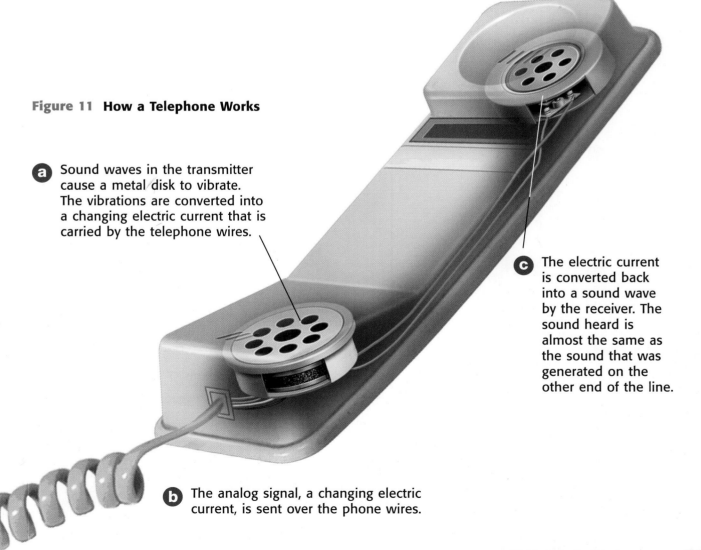

a Sound waves in the transmitter cause a metal disk to vibrate. The vibrations are converted into a changing electric current that is carried by the telephone wires.

c The electric current is converted back into a sound wave by the receiver. The sound heard is almost the same as the sound that was generated on the other end of the line.

b The analog signal, a changing electric current, is sent over the phone wires.

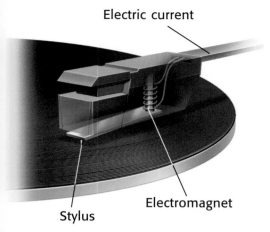

Electric current

Electromagnet

Stylus

Figure 12 *As the stylus rides in the record's grooves, it causes an electromagnet to vibrate.*

Analog Recording One way to reproduce sound is by storing an analog signal of the sound wave. In vinyl records, the analog signal is carved into a grooved plastic disk. The frequency and loudness of the sound are represented by the number and depth of the contours carved into the grooved disk.

Playing a Record **Figure 12** shows how a record player's needle, called a stylus (STIE luhs), creates vibrations in an electromagnet. The vibrating electromagnet creates an electric current that is used to produce sound. Although analog recording produces sound that is very similar to the original sound, it has some drawbacks. First, undesirable sounds are sometimes recorded and are difficult to filter out. Also, because the stylus physically touches the record to play it, records can wear out, so the sound can be changed over time.

Digital Signals

A **digital signal** is a series of electric pulses that represents the digits of binary (BIE neh ree) numbers. *Binary* means two. A series of digits, which are composed of only two numbers—1 and 0—represent binary numbers. Each pulse in a digital signal stands for a 1, and each missing pulse is a 0.

Digital Storage on a CD You've probably listened to the digital sound from a compact disc, or CD. Sound is recorded onto a CD by means of a digital signal. A CD stores digital signals in a thin layer of aluminum. As shown in **Figure 13,** the aluminum layer has a series of pits. Each pit is a 0, and each nonpitted region, called a land, is a 1.

Figure 13 *Pits and lands form a tight spiral from the center to the outer edge on a CD. They store information that can be converted by a CD player into sound.*

Label   Protective coating   Aluminum   Plastic

Land

Pit

Digital Recording In a digital recording, the amplitude of the sound wave is sampled many times per second. From the samples, numbers are generated that are equal to the amplitude of the sound at each instant. **Figure 14** shows how these sample values represent the original sound signal. These numbers are then represented in binary as 1s and 0s and stored as pits and lands on a CD. Undesirable sample values can be filtered out, resulting in a cleaner sound.

The drawback to digital recording is that the sample values don't exactly match the original sound wave. To improve the reproduction of sound, a higher sampling rate can be used. A higher sampling rate means that there will be more sample values taken each second (narrower bars), and the resulting digital sound will be closer to the original sound.

Playing a CD In a CD player, the CD spins around while a laser scans it from underneath. As shown in **Figure 15,** the detector in a CD player receives light reflected from the surface of the CD. The detector converts the pattern of reflected light into a digital signal. The digital signal is changed into an analog signal, which is used to generate a sound wave. Because only light touches the CD, the CD doesn't wear out even after it has been played many times.

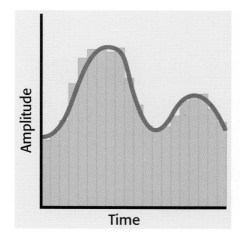

Figure 14 *Each bar represents a digital sample of the sound wave.*

Figure 15 *Different sequences and sizes of pits and lands will register different patterns of numbers that are converted into different sounds.*

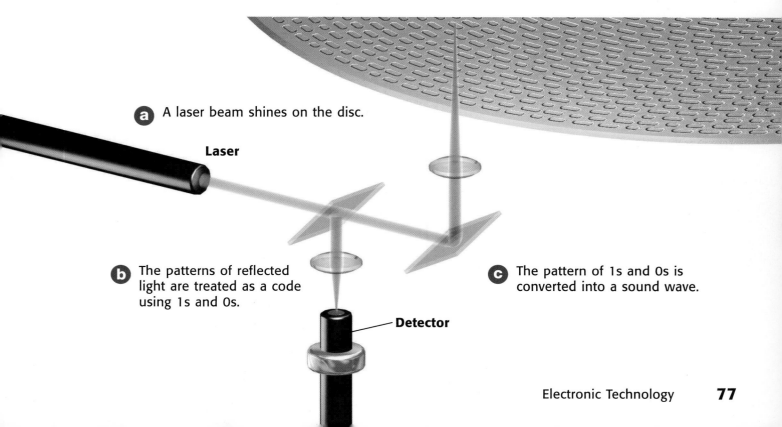

a A laser beam shines on the disc.

Laser

b The patterns of reflected light are treated as a code using 1s and 0s.

c The pattern of 1s and 0s is converted into a sound wave.

Detector

Radio and Television

When you turn on your radio or television, you can hear or see programs broadcast from a radio or TV station that may be many kilometers away. Radio and television use electromagnetic waves. An *electromagnetic wave* is a wave that consists of changing electric and magnetic fields.

Radio Radio waves are one type of electromagnetic wave. The basic operation of a radio involves using radio waves to carry signals that represent sound. As shown in **Figure 16,** radio waves are transmitted by a radio tower, travel through the air, and are picked up by a radio antenna.

Get tuned in! Turn to page 100 in the LabBook, and build your own radio-wave receiver.

Figure 16 How Radio Works

1 A microphone creates an electric current that is an analog signal of the original sound wave.

2 A modulator combines the amplified analog signal with radio waves that have a specific frequency.

3 A radio tower transmits modulated radio waves through the air.

4 The antenna in a radio "tuned in" to the correct frequency receives the modulated radio waves. The receiver removes the radio waves from the analog signal.

5 The radio's speakers convert the analog signal, the electric current, into sound.

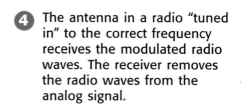

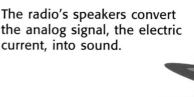

Television The images you see on your television are produced by beams of electrons projected onto a screen. Three beams of electrons are produced within a cathode-ray tube, or CRT. The screen is coated with special fluorescent (FLOO uh RES uhnt) materials that glow when hit by electrons. Video signals, which contain the information that produces an image, are carried by electromagnetic waves. Electromagnetic waves also carry the audio signals that produce sound from the speakers. Look at **Figure 17** to learn how a color television works.

Activity

Use a magnifying lens to look at a television screen. How are the fluorescent materials arranged? Hold the lens at various distances from the screen. What effects do you see? How does the screen's changing picture affect what you see?

TRY at HOME

Figure 17 Images on a Color Television

1 Video signals transmitted from a TV station are received by the antenna of a TV receiver.

2 Electronic circuits separate the video signal into separate signals for each of three electron beams. The beams, one for each primary color of light (red, green, and blue), strike the screen in varying strengths determined by the video signal.

3 Three fluorescent materials (each corresponding to an electron beam) are arranged in stripes or dots on the screen. The electron beams sweep the screen to activate the fluorescent materials. These materials then emit colored light that is viewed as a picture.

SECTION REVIEW

1. How are analog signals different from digital signals?

2. Compare how a telephone and a radio tower transmit information.

3. **Making Predictions** How could a digital signal be corrupted?

internet**connect**

SCiLINKS
NSTA

TOPIC: Telephone Technology, Television Technology
GO TO: www.scilinks.org
*sci*LINKS NUMBER: HSTP460, HSTP465

Terms to Learn

computer
microprocessor
hardware
software
Internet

What You'll Do

◆ List the basic functions of a computer.
◆ Identify the main components of computer hardware.
◆ Describe what computer software allows a computer to do.
◆ Describe how the Internet works.

Computers

Did you use a computer to wake up this morning? You might think of a computer as something you use to send e-mail or surf the Net, but computers are around you all the time. Computers are in automobiles, VCRs, and telephones. Even an alarm clock is a computer! An alarm clock, like the one in **Figure 18,** lets you program the time you want to wake up, and will wake you up at that time.

Figure 18 *Believe it or not, this alarm clock is a computer!*

What Is a Computer?

A **computer** is an electronic device that performs tasks by processing and storing information. A computer performs a task when it is given a command and has the instructions necessary to carry out that command. Computers do not operate by themselves, or "think."

Basic Functions The basic functions a computer performs are shown in **Figure 19.** The information you give to a computer is called *input.* Setting your alarm clock is a type of input. To perform a task, a computer *processes* the input, changing it to a desirable form. Processing could mean adding a list of numbers, executing a drawing, or even moving a piece of equipment. Input doesn't have to be processed immediately; it can also be stored until it is needed. Computers store information in their *memory.* For example, your alarm clock stores the time you want to wake up. It can then process this stored information by going off when it is the programmed time. *Output* is the final result of the task performed by the computer. What's the output of an alarm clock? The sound that wakes you up!

Figure 19
The Functions of a Computer

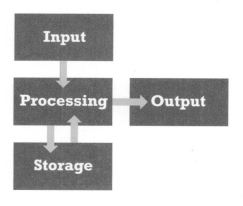

Historic Developments

Your pocket calculator is a simple example of a computer. But computers weren't always so small and efficient. The first computers were massive systems consisting of large pieces of electronic equipment that could fill up an entire room.

The First Computers The first general-purpose computer is shown in **Figure 20.** This monstrous collection of equipment is the ENIAC (Electronic Numerical Integrator and Computer), developed in 1946 by the U.S. Army. The ENIAC consisted of thousands of vacuum tubes and, as a result, produced a lot of excess thermal energy. It was also extremely expensive to build and maintain.

BRAIN FOOD

When the ENIAC was built, transistors and integrated circuits did not exist. Instead, it used 18,000 vacuum tubes, filled a 10 × 15.25 m room, had a mass of more than 23,500 kg, and used as much electrical energy as 150 ordinary light bulbs!

Figure 20 *Fast for its time, the ENIAC could add 5,000 numbers per second.*

Modern Computers With the invention of transistors and integrated circuits, the size of computers could be greatly reduced. Computers today use microprocessors, like the one shown in **Figure 21.** A **microprocessor** is an integrated circuit that contains many of a computer's capabilities on a single silicon chip. The first commercially available microprocessor contained only 4,800 transistors, but microprocessors made today may contain more than 3 million transistors. As a result, computers can now be made so small and lightweight that we can carry them around like a notebook!

Figure 21 *This microprocessor is about 4 × 4 cm.*

Computer Hardware

For each function of a computer, there is a corresponding part of the computer where each function occurs. **Hardware** refers to the parts or equipment that make up a computer. As you read about each piece of hardware, refer to **Figure 22.**

Input Devices Instructions given to a computer are called input. An *input device* is the piece of hardware that feeds information to the computer. You can enter information into a computer using a keyboard, a mouse, a scanner, a digitizing pad and pen—even your own voice!

Central Processing Unit A computer performs tasks within an area called the *central processing unit,* or CPU. In a personal computer, the CPU is a microprocessor. Input goes through the CPU for immediate processing or for storage in memory. The CPU is where the computer does calculations, solves problems, and executes the instructions given to it.

Figure 22 Computer Hardware

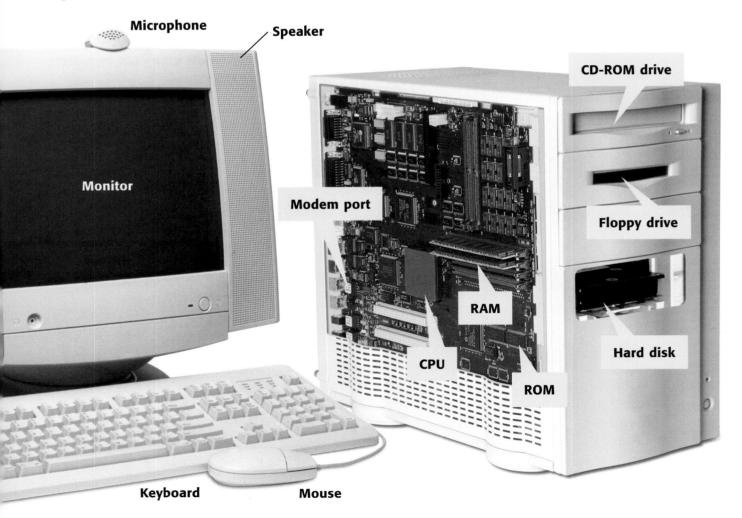

Memory Information can be stored in the computer's memory until it is needed. Hard disks inside a computer and floppy disks or CD-ROMs inserted into a computer have memory to store information. Two other types of memory are *ROM* (read-only memory) and *RAM* (random-access memory).

ROM is permanent. It handles functions such as computer start-up, maintenance, and hardware management. ROM normally cannot be added to or changed, and it cannot be lost when the computer is turned off. On the other hand, RAM is temporary. It stores information only while that information is being used. RAM is sometimes called working memory. Large amounts of RAM allow more information to be input, which makes for a more powerful computer.

Output Devices Once a computer performs a task, it shows the results on an *output device*. Monitors, printers, and speaker systems are all examples of output devices.

Modems One piece of computer hardware that serves as an input device as well as an output device is a *modem*. Modems allow computers to communicate. One computer can input information into another computer over a telephone line, as long as each computer has its own modem. As a result, modems permit computers to "talk" with other computers.

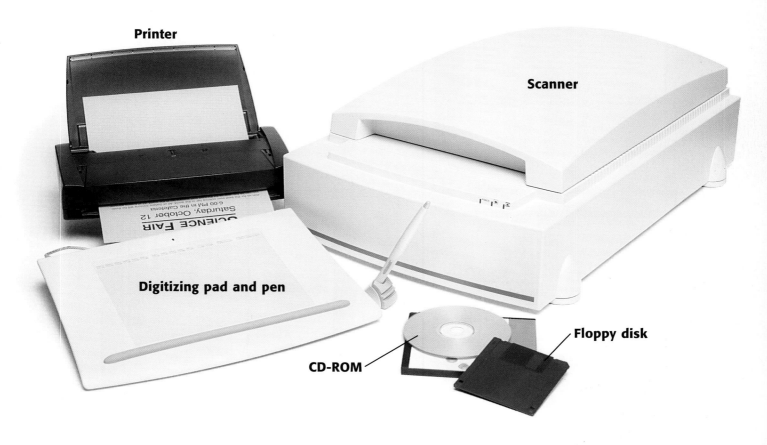

Printer

Scanner

Digitizing pad and pen

CD-ROM

Floppy disk

Computer Software

Computers need a set of instructions before they can perform any given task. **Software** is a set of instructions, or commands, that tells a computer what to do. A computer program is an example of software.

Kinds of Software Software can be classified into two categories: operating system software and application software. Operating system software manages basic operations required by the computer and supervises all interactions between software and hardware. It interprets commands from the input device, such as locating programming instructions on a hard disk to be loaded into memory.

Application software contains instructions ordering the computer to operate a utility, such as a word processor, spreadsheet, or even a computer game. The pages in this book were created using a variety of application software! Some examples of application software are shown in **Figure 23.**

Figure 23 *Computer software allows a computer to perform all kinds of tasks, such as word processing, video games, interactive tutoring, and graphics.*

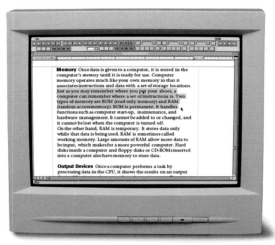

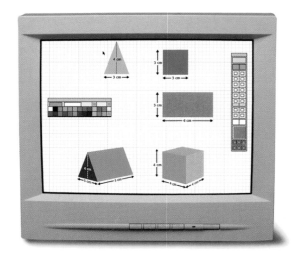

The Internet—A Global Network

Thanks to modems and computer software, it is possible to connect many computers and allow them to communicate with one another. That's what the **Internet** is—a huge computer network consisting of millions of computers that can all share information with one another.

How the Internet Works Computers can connect to one another on the Internet by using modems to dial into an Internet Service Provider, or ISP. A home computer connects to an ISP over a normal phone line. A school, business, or other group can have a Local Area Network (LAN) that connects to an ISP using one phone line. As depicted in **Figure 24,** ISPs are connected globally by satellite. And that's how computers go global!

Figure 24 *Through a series of connections like this, every computer on the Internet can share information.*

SECTION REVIEW

1. Using the terms *input, output, processing,* and *memory,* explain how you use a pocket calculator to add numbers.

2. What is the difference between hardware and software?

3. **Analyzing Relationships** Could something like the Internet exist without modems and telephone lines? Explain.

Chapter Highlights

Vocabulary

circuit board (p. 68)
semiconductor (p. 69)
doping (p. 69)
diode (p. 70)
transistor (p. 71)
integrated circuit (p. 72)

Section Notes

• Electronic devices use electrical energy to transmit information.

• Many electronic components are made of semiconductors. Two types of semiconductors result from a process called doping. They are n-type and p-type semiconductors.

• The two types of semiconductors can be sandwiched together to produce diodes and transistors.

• Diodes allow electric current in only one direction.

• Transistors can be used as amplifiers or as switches.

• Integrated circuits can contain many electronic components. They allow electronic systems to be smaller.

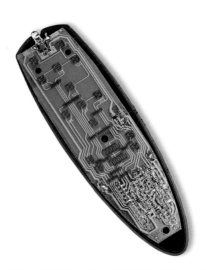

Vocabulary

telecommunication (p. 74)
signal (p. 74)
analog signal (p. 75)
digital signal (p. 76)

Section Notes

• Electronic devices use signals to transmit information. The signals are usually contained in another form of energy, such as radio waves or electric current.

• The properties of analog signals change continuously according to changes in the original signal. Telephones use analog signals.

• A digital signal is a series of electrical pulses that represents the digits of binary numbers. CD players use digital signals.

☑ Skills Check

Visual Understanding

DIODES Sandwiching an n-type semiconductor and a p-type semiconductor together produces a diode. Charges can pass through a diode in only one direction.

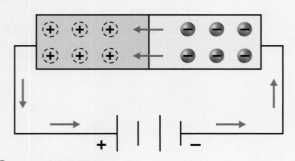

TRANSMITTING SIGNALS BY RADIO
Electronic devices transmit information through signals. Look at Figure 16 on page 78 to see how electromagnetic waves can transmit radio signals.

COMPUTERS In order for a computer to perform a task, it must be given information. Look at the diagram on page 80 to learn about the steps a computer takes to perform various tasks.

SECTION 2

- Sound can be recorded digitally or as an analog signal.

- Radio and television rely on electromagnetic waves.

- In radio, signals that represent sound are combined with radio waves and sent through the air. Radios can pick up the radio waves and convert them back to sound waves.

- A color television image is produced by three electron beams that scan the screen of a cathode-ray tube, or CRT. Fluorescent materials on the screen glow to create the picture.

Labs
Tune In! *(p. 100)*

SECTION 3

Vocabulary
computer *(p. 80)*

microprocessor *(p. 81)*

hardware *(p. 82)*

software *(p. 84)*

Internet *(p. 85)*

Section Notes

- The basic functions of a computer involve input, processing, memory, and output. A computer cannot perform a task without a set of commands.

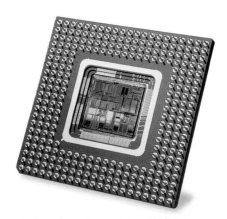

- The first computers were very large and could not perform many tasks.

- Because microprocessors contain many computer capabilities on a single chip, computers have been reduced in size.

- Computer hardware refers to the parts or the equipment that make up a computer.

- Computer software is a set of instructions or commands that tells a computer what to do.

- Modems allow millions of computers to connect with one another and share information on the Internet.

Chapter Review

USING VOCABULARY

For each pair of terms, explain the difference in their meanings.

1. semiconductor/doping

2. transistor/diode

3. signal/telecommunication

4. analog signal/digital signal

5. computer/microprocessor

6. hardware/software

UNDERSTANDING CONCEPTS

Multiple Choice

7. All electronic devices transmit information using
   a. signals.
   b. electromagnetic waves.
   c. radio waves.
   d. modems.

8. Semiconductors are used to make
   a. transistors.
   b. integrated circuits.
   c. diodes.
   d. All of the above

9. Which of the following is an example of a telecommunication device?
   a. vacuum tube
   b. telephone
   c. radio
   d. Both (b) and (c)

10. A monitor, printer, and speaker are examples of
    a. input devices.   c. computers.
    b. memory.   d. output devices.

11. Record players play sounds that were recorded in the form of
    a. digital signals.
    b. electric current.
    c. analog signals.
    d. radio waves.

12. Memory in a computer that is permanent and cannot be added to is called
    a. RAM.
    b. ROM.
    c. CPU.
    d. None of the above

13. Cathode-ray tubes are used in
    a. telephones.
    b. telegraphs.
    c. televisions.
    d. radios.

Short Answer

14. How is an electronic device different from a machine that uses electrical energy?

15. How does a diode allow current to flow in one direction?

16. In one or two sentences, describe how a TV works.

17. Give three examples of how computers are used in your everyday life.

18. Explain the advantages that transistors have over vacuum tubes.

Concept Mapping

19. Use the following terms to create a concept map: electronic devices, radio waves, electric current, signals, information.

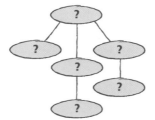

CRITICAL THINKING AND PROBLEM SOLVING

20. Your friend is preparing an oral report on the history of radio and finds the photograph shown below. "Why is this radio so huge?" he asks you. Using what you know about electronic devices, how do you explain the size of this vintage radio?

21. Using what you know about the differences between analog and digital signals, explain how the sound from a record player is different from the sound from a CD player.

22. What do Morse code and digital signals have in common?

23. Computers can process a lot of information, but they cannot think. Explain why this is true.

24. Based on what you learned in the chapter, how do you think an automatic garage door opener works?

INTERPRETING GRAPHICS

Look at the diagram below, and answer the questions that follow.

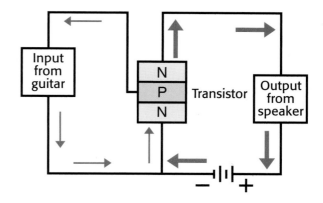

25. What purpose does the transistor serve in this situation?

26. How does the current in the left side of the circuit compare with the current in the right side of the circuit?

27. How does the sound from the speaker compare with the sound from the guitar?

Reading Check-up Take a minute to review your answers to the Pre-Reading Questions found at the bottom of page 66. Have your answers changed? If necessary, revise your answers based on what you have learned since you began this chapter.

Listening Lower

Do you ever listen to your favorite music on headphones? Many people like to use headphones while they exercise. Terrific! But doctors believe that this habit may be putting people's hearing at risk.

The Blood Brain Drain

Aerobic exercise, including walking, jogging, skating, dancing, and competitive sports, is an important part of a healthy lifestyle. However, when you exercise, more blood is sent to your arms and legs than is sent to your ears. The inner ear is more easily damaged when the blood flow is lowered. Once the cells of the inner ear are damaged, they cannot be replaced. A study in Sweden showed that hearing loss doubles when loud noise and aerobic exercise are combined!

How Loud Is Too Loud?

The federal Occupational Safety and Health Administration (OSHA) requires hearing protection for workers exposed to 95 decibels for 4 hours. A lawn mower emits 95 decibels. If workers are exposed to 100 decibels for 3 hours, they must wear hearing protection. People generally listen to headphones at levels between 90 and 115 decibels.

Why So Loud?

Most people turn the volume up as they continue to listen to music because their ears adapt to the volume. However, permanent hearing

▲ *How high should the volume be when listening to music on headphones?*

loss can occur at well below painful or even uncomfortable levels. Another concern is that hearing loss is often gradual, starting at high frequencies. The loss goes unnoticed until the damage is quite extensive. Generally, more problems occur when noise is louder, lasts longer, or occurs frequently.

What to Do

How can you protect your hearing and still use those headphones? Keep the volume of your headphones as low as possible, and try not to raise the volume once it is set. Then always remember this: If a person 1 m away has to shout in order for you to hear, the volume is too high. However, this test does not work for headphones with muffs that fit around the ear. The volume is probably too high if your hearing is dulled after you remove your headphones. This usually goes away quickly, but it may become permanent if you keep the volume high.

Sound It Out

► Obtain a sound meter, and survey the sound levels around your school. Measure the levels at dances and other noisy locations. Report your findings to your class, and discuss ways to lower your exposure to loud sounds. You may just save someone's hearing!

Science Fiction

Once upo...
in a farawa...
land...
there
lived a
space

who had a
...tic ship
...f silver
...great
haircut that
was the galax...

"There Will Come Soft Rains"

by Ray Bradbury

Ticktock, *seven o'clock, time to get up, time to get up, seven o'clock.* The voice clock in the living room sends out the wake-up message, gently calling to the family to get up and begin their new day.

It is August 4, 2026, in Allandale, California. The house is attractive, in an attractive neighborhood, just right for a mother, father, two children, and a dog. And it is state of the art: automatic kitchen, extremely sensitive fire-detection and fire-protection systems, walls that look like walls but become video display screens—everything a family could want.

A few minutes after the wake-up call, the automatic stove in the kitchen begins the family breakfast—toast, eggs (sunny side up), and bacon. While the breakfast is cooking, the voice in the kitchen ceiling lists the reminders for the day: a birthday, an anniversary, the bills that are due.

About an hour after the wake-up message, the ceiling voice speaks again, this time to remind anyone listening that it is time to go to school. A soft rain is falling outside, so the weather box by the front door suggests that raincoats are necessary today.

But something has happened. No family sounds come from the house. The house goes on talking to itself and carrying on its routine as if it were keeping itself company. Why doesn't anyone answer? Find out when you read Ray Bradbury's "There Will Come Soft Rains" in the *Holt Anthology of Science Fiction*.

SAFETY FIRST!

Exploring, inventing, and investigating are essential to the study of science. However, these activities can also be dangerous. To make sure that your experiments and explorations are safe, you must be aware of a variety of safety guidelines.

You have probably heard of the saying, "It is better to be safe than sorry." This is particularly true in a science classroom where experiments and explorations are being performed. Being uninformed and careless can result in serious injuries. Don't take chances with your own safety or with anyone else's.

Following are important guidelines for staying safe in the science classroom. Your teacher may also have safety guidelines and tips that are specific to your classroom and laboratory. Take the time to be safe.

Safety Rules!

Start Out Right

Always get your teacher's permission before attempting any laboratory exploration. Read the procedures carefully, and pay particular attention to safety information and caution statements. If you are unsure about what a safety symbol means, look it up or ask your teacher. You cannot be too careful when it comes to safety. If an accident does occur, inform your teacher immediately, regardless of how minor you think the accident is.

Safety Symbols

All of the experiments and investigations in this book and their related worksheets include important safety symbols to alert you to particular safety concerns. Become familiar with these symbols so that when you see them, you will know what they mean and what to do. It is important that you read this entire safety section to learn about specific dangers in the laboratory.

If you are instructed to note the odor of a substance, wave the fumes toward your nose with your hand. Never put your nose close to the source.

Eye protection

Clothing protection

Hand safety

Heating safety

Electric safety

Chemical safety

Animal safety

Sharp object

Plant safety

Eye Safety

Wear safety goggles when working around chemicals, acids, bases, or any type of flame or heating device. Wear safety goggles any time there is even the slightest chance that harm could come to your eyes. If any substance gets into your eyes, notify your teacher immediately, and flush your eyes with running water for at least 15 minutes. Treat any unknown chemical as if it were a dangerous chemical. Never look directly into the sun. Doing so could cause permanent blindness.

Avoid wearing contact lenses in a laboratory situation. Even if you are wearing safety goggles, chemicals can get between the contact lenses and your eyes. If your doctor requires that you wear contact lenses instead of glasses, wear eye-cup safety goggles in the lab.

Safety Equipment

Know the locations of the nearest fire alarms and any other safety equipment, such as fire blankets and eyewash fountains, as identified by your teacher, and know the procedures for using them.

Be extra careful when using any glassware. When adding a heavy object to a graduated cylinder, tilt the cylinder so the object slides slowly to the bottom.

Neatness

Keep your work area free of all unnecessary books and papers. Tie back long hair, and secure loose sleeves or other loose articles of clothing, such as ties and bows. Remove dangling jewelry. Don't wear open-toed shoes or sandals in the laboratory. Never eat, drink, or apply cosmetics in a laboratory setting. Food, drink, and cosmetics can easily become contaminated with dangerous materials.

Certain hair products (such as aerosol hair spray) are flammable and should not be worn while working near an open flame. Avoid wearing hair spray or hair gel on lab days.

Sharp/Pointed Objects

Use knives and other sharp instruments with extreme care. Never cut objects while holding them in your hands. Place objects on a suitable work surface for cutting.

Heat

Wear safety goggles when using a heating device or a flame. Whenever possible, use an electric hot plate as a heat source instead of an open flame. When heating materials in a test tube, always angle the test tube away from yourself and others. In order to avoid burns, wear heat-resistant gloves whenever instructed to do so.

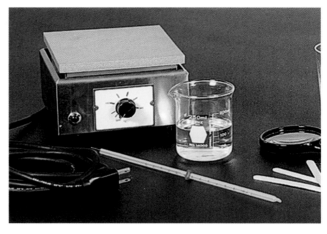

Chemicals

Wear safety goggles when handling any potentially dangerous chemicals, acids, or bases. If a chemical is unknown, handle it as you would a dangerous chemical. Wear an apron and safety gloves when working with acids or bases or whenever you are told to do so. If a spill gets on your skin or clothing, rinse it off immediately with water for at least 5 minutes while calling to your teacher.

Never mix chemicals unless your teacher tells you to do so. Never taste, touch, or smell chemicals unless you are specifically directed to do so. Before working with a flammable liquid or gas, check for the presence of any source of flame, spark, or heat.

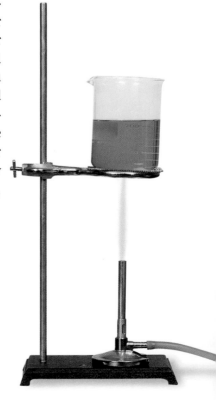

Electricity

Be careful with electrical cords. When using a microscope with a lamp, do not place the cord where it could trip someone. Do not let cords hang over a table edge in a way that could cause equipment to fall if the cord is accidentally pulled. Do not use equipment with damaged cords. Be sure your hands are dry and that the electrical equipment is in the "off" position before plugging it in. Turn off and unplug electrical equipment when you are finished.

Animal Safety

Always obtain your teacher's permission before bringing any animal into the school building. Handle animals only as your teacher directs. Always treat animals carefully and with respect. Wash your hands thoroughly after handling any animal.

Plant Safety

Do not eat any part of a plant or plant seed used in the laboratory. Wash hands thoroughly after handling any part of a plant. When in nature, do not pick any wild plants unless your teacher instructs you to do so.

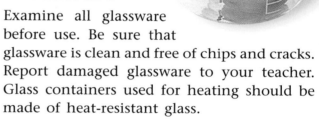

Glassware

Examine all glassware before use. Be sure that glassware is clean and free of chips and cracks. Report damaged glassware to your teacher. Glass containers used for heating should be made of heat-resistant glass.

DISCOVERY LAB

Stop the Static Electricity!

Imagine this scenario: Some of your clothes cling together when they come out of the dryer. This annoying problem is caused by static electricity—the buildup of electric charges on an object. In this lab, you'll discover how this buildup occurs.

Materials

- 30 cm thread
- plastic-foam packing peanut
- tape
- rubber rod
- wool cloth
- glass rod
- silk cloth

Ask a Question

1. How do electric charges build up on clothes in a dryer?

Form a Hypothesis

2. Write a statement that answers the question above. Explain your reasoning.

Test the Hypothesis

3. Tie a piece of thread approximately 30 cm in length to a packing peanut. Hang the peanut by the thread from the edge of a table. Tape the thread to the table.

4. Rub the rubber rod with the wool cloth for 10–15 seconds. Bring the rod near, but do not touch, the peanut. Observe the peanut and record your observations. If nothing happens, repeat this step.

5. Touch the peanut with the rubber rod. Pull the rod away from the peanut, and then bring it near again. Record your observations.

6. Repeat steps 4 and 5 with the glass rod and silk cloth.

7. Now rub the rubber rod with the wool cloth, and bring the rod near the peanut again. Record your observations.

Analyze the Results

8. What caused the peanut to act differently in steps 4 and 5?

9. Did the glass rod have the same effect on the peanut as the rubber rod did? Explain how the peanut reacted in each case.

10. Was the reaction of the peanut the same in steps 5 and 7? Explain.

Draw Conclusions

11. Based on your results, was your hypothesis correct? Explain your answer, and write a new statement if necessary.

Communicate Results

12. Explain why the rubber rod and the glass rod affected the peanut.

Going Further

Do some research to find out how a dryer sheet helps stop the buildup of electric charges in the dryer.

Potato Power

Have you ever wanted to look inside a D cell from a flashlight or an AA cell from a portable radio? All cells include the same basic components, as shown below. There is a metal "bucket," some electrolyte (a paste), and a rod of some other metal (or solid) in the middle. Even though the construction is simple, companies that manufacture cells are always trying to make a product with the highest voltage possible from the least expensive materials. Sometimes they try different pastes, and sometimes they try different combinations of metals. In this lab, you will make your own cell. Using inexpensive materials, you will try to produce the highest voltage you can.

Materials

- labeled metal strips
- potato
- metric ruler
- voltmeter

Procedure

1. Choose two metal strips. Carefully push one of the strips into the potato at least 2 cm deep. Insert the second strip the same way, and measure how far apart the two strips are. (If one of your metal strips is too soft to push into the potato, push a harder strip in first, remove it, and then push the soft strip into the slit.) Record the two metals you have used and the distance between the strips in your ScienceLog. **Caution:** The strips of metal may have sharp edges.

2. Connect the voltmeter to the two strips, and record the voltage.

3. Move one of the strips closer to or farther from the other. Measure the new distance and voltage. Record your results.

4. Repeat steps 1 through 3, using different combinations of metal strips and distances until you find the combination that produces the highest voltage.

Analysis

5. What combination of metals and distance produced the highest voltage?

6. If you change only the distance but use the same metal strips, what is the effect on the voltage?

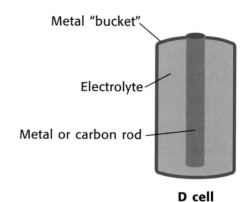

Metal "bucket"

Electrolyte

Metal or carbon rod

D cell

7. One of the metal strips tends to lose electrons, while the other tends to gain electrons. What do you think would happen if you used two strips of the same metal?

Build a DC Motor

Electric motors can be used for many things. Hair dryers, CD players, and even some cars and buses are powered by electric motors. In this lab, you will build a direct current electric motor—the basis for the electric motors you use every day.

Materials

- 100 cm of magnet wire
- cardboard tube
- sandpaper
- 2 large paper clips
- 4 disk magnets
- plastic-foam cup
- tape
- 2 insulated wires with alligator clips, each approximately 30 cm long
- 4.5 V battery
- permanent marker

Procedure

1. To make the armature for the motor, wind the wire around the cardboard tube to make a coil like the one shown below. Wind the ends of the wire around the loops on each side of the coil. Leave about 5 cm free on each end.

2. Hold the coil on its edge. Sand the enamel from only the top half of each end of the wire. This acts like a commutator, except that it blocks the electric current instead of reversing it during half of each rotation.

3. Partially unfold the two paper clips from the middle. Make a hook in one end of each paper clip to hold the coil, as shown at right.

4. Place two disk magnets in the bottom of the cup, and place the other magnets on the outside of the bottom of the cup. The magnets should remain in place when the cup is turned upside down.

5. Tape the paper clips to the sides of the cup. The hooks should be at the same height, and should keep the coil from hitting the magnet.

6. Test your coil. Flick the top of the coil lightly with your finger. The coil should spin freely without wobbling or sliding to one side.

7. Make adjustments to the ends of the wire and the hooks until your coil spins freely.

8. Use the alligator clips to attach one wire to each paper clip.

9. Attach the free end of one wire to one terminal of the battery.

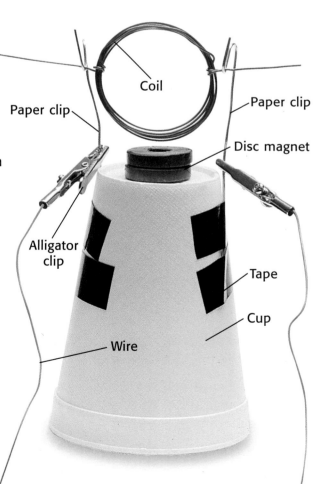

Coil

Paper clip

Paper clip

Disc magnet

Alligator clip

Tape

Cup

Wire

Collect Data

10. Connect the free end of the other wire to the second battery terminal and give your coil a gentle spin. Record your observations.

11. Stop the coil and give it a gentle spin in the opposite direction. Record your observations.

12. If the coil does not keep spinning, check the ends of the wire. Bare wire should touch the paper clips during half of the spin, and only enamel should touch the paper clips for the other half of the spin.

13. If you removed too much enamel, color half of the wire with a permanent marker.

14. Switch the connections to the battery and repeat steps 10 and 11.

Analyze the Results

15. Did your motor always spin in the direction you started it? Explain.

16. Why was the motor affected by switching the battery connections?

17. Some electric cars run on solar power. Which part of your model would be replaced by the solar panels?

Draw Conclusions

18. Some people claim that electric-powered cars are cleaner than gasoline-powered cars. Explain why this might be true.

19. List some reasons that electric cars are not ideal. (Hint: What happens to batteries?)

20. How could your model be used to help design a hair dryer?

21. Make a list of at least three other items that could be powered by an electric motor like the one you built.

Tune In!

You probably have listened to radios many times in your life. Modern radios are complicated electronic devices. However, radios do not have to be so complicated. The basic parts of all radios include: a diode, an inductor, a capacitor, an antenna, a ground wire, and an earphone (or a speaker and amplifier on a large radio). In this activity, you will examine each of these components one at a time as you build a working model of a radio-wave receiver.

Materials

- diode
- 2 m of insulated wire
- 2 cardboard tubes
- tape
- scissors
- aluminum foil
- sheet of paper
- 7 connecting wires, 30 cm each
- 3 paper clips
- cardboard, 20 × 30 cm
- antenna
- ground wire
- earphone

Procedure

1. Examine the diode. Describe it in your ScienceLog.

2. A diode carries current in only one direction. Draw the inside of a diode in your ScienceLog, and illustrate how this might occur.

3. An inductor controls the amount of electric current due to the resistance of the wire. Make an inductor by winding the insulated wire around a cardboard tube approximately 100 times. Wind the wire so that all the turns of the coil are neat and in an orderly row, as shown below. Leave about 25 cm of wire on each end of the coil. The coil of wire may be held on the tube using tape.

4. Now you will construct the variable capacitor. A capacitor stores electrical energy when an electric current is applied. A variable capacitor is a capacitor in which the amount of energy stored can be changed. Cut a piece of aluminum foil to go around the tube but only half the length of the tube, as shown on the next page. Keep the foil as wrinkle-free as possible as you wrap it around the tube, and tape the foil to itself. Now tape the foil to the tube.

5. Use the sheet of paper and tape to make a sliding cover on the tube. The paper should completely cover the foil on the tube with about 1 cm extra.

6. Cut another sheet of aluminum foil to wrap completely around the paper. Leave approximately 1 cm of paper showing at each end of the foil. Tape this foil sheet to the paper sleeve. If you have done this correctly, you have a paper/foil sheet which will slide up and down the tube over the stationary foil. The two pieces of foil should not touch.

7. Stand your variable capacitor on its end so that the stationary foil is at the bottom. The amount of stored energy is greater when the sleeve is down than when the sleeve is up.

8. Use tape to attach one connecting wire to the stationary foil at the end of the tube. Use tape to attach another connecting wire to the sliding foil sleeve. Be sure that the metal part of the wire touches the foil.

9. Hook three paper clips on one edge of the cardboard, as shown below. Label one paper clip A, another B, and the third one C.

10. Lay the inductor on the piece of cardboard, and tape it to the cardboard.

11. Stand the capacitor next to the inductor, and tape the tube to the cardboard. Be sure not to tape the sleeve—it must be free to slide.

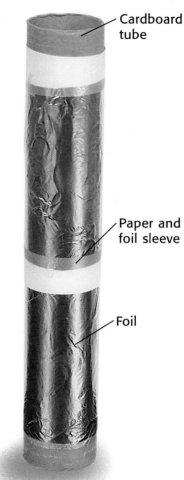

Cardboard tube

Paper and foil sleeve

Foil

Capacitor

Partially Completed Model Receiver

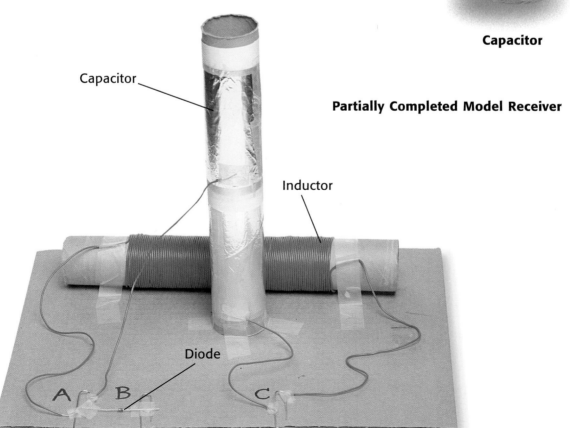

Capacitor

Inductor

Diode

A B C

12. Use tape to connect the diode to paper clips A and B. The cathode should be closest to paper clip B. (The cathode end of the diode is the one with the dark band.) Make sure that all connections have good metal-to-metal contact.

13. Connect one end of the inductor to paper clip A, and the other end to paper clip C. Use tape to hold the wires in place.

14. Connect the wire from the sliding part of the capacitor to paper clip A. Connect the other wire (from the stationary foil) to paper clip C.

15. The antenna receives radio waves transmitted by a radio station. Tape a connecting wire to your antenna. Then connect this wire to paper clip A.

16. Use tape to connect one end of the ground wire to paper clip C. The other end of the ground wire should be connected to an object specified by your teacher.

A Completed Model Receiver!

Earphone

Antenna

Ground wire

17. The earphone will allow you to detect the radio waves you receive. Connect one wire from the earphone to paper clip B and the other wire to paper clip C.

18. You are now ready to begin listening. With everything connected, and the earphone in your ear, slowly slide the paper/foil sheet of the capacitor up and down. Listen for a very faint sound. You may have to troubleshoot many of the parts to get your receiver to work. As you troubleshoot, check to be sure there is good contact between all the connections.

Analysis

19. Describe the process of operating your receiver.

20. Considering what you have learned about a diode, why is it important to have the diode connected the correct way?

21. A function of the inductor on a radio is to "slow the current down." Why does the inductor you made slow the current down more than does a straight wire the length of your coil?

22. A capacitor consists of any two conductors separated by an insulator. For your capacitor, list the two conductors and the insulator.

23. Explain why the amount of stored energy is increased when you slide the foil sleeve down and decreased when the sleeve is up.

24. In your ScienceLog, make a list of ways that your receiver is similar to a modern radio. Make a second list of ways that your receiver is different from a modern radio.

Concept Mapping: A Way to Bring Ideas Together

What Is a Concept Map?

Have you ever tried to tell someone about a book or a chapter you've just read and found that you can remember only a few isolated words and ideas? Or maybe you've memorized facts for a test and then weeks later discovered you're not even sure what topics those facts covered.

In both cases, you may have understood the ideas or concepts by themselves but not in relation to one another. If you could somehow link the ideas together, you would probably understand them better and remember them longer. This is something a concept map can help you do. A concept map is a way to see how ideas or concepts fit together. It can help you see the "big picture."

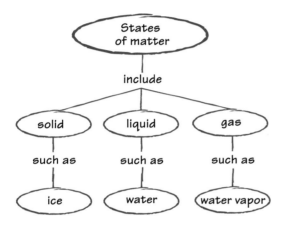

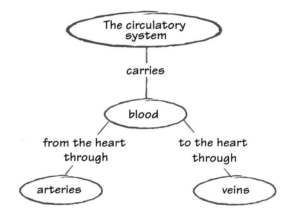

How to Make a Concept Map

❶ Make a list of the main ideas or concepts.

It might help to write each concept on its own slip of paper. This will make it easier to rearrange the concepts as many times as necessary to make sense of how the concepts are connected. After you've made a few concept maps this way, you can go directly from writing your list to actually making the map.

❷ Arrange the concepts in order from the most general to the most specific.

Put the most general concept at the top and circle it. Ask yourself, "How does this concept relate to the remaining concepts?" As you see the relationships, arrange the concepts in order from general to specific.

❸ Connect the related concepts with lines.

❹ On each line, write an action word or short phrase that shows how the concepts are related.

Look at the concept maps on this page, and then see if you can make one for the following terms:

plants, water, photosynthesis, carbon dioxide, sun's energy

One possible answer is provided at right, but don't look at it until you try the concept map yourself.

SI Measurement

The International System of Units, or SI, is the standard system of measurement used by many scientists. Using the same standards of measurement makes it easier for scientists to communicate with one another.

SI works by combining prefixes and base units. Each base unit can be used with different prefixes to define smaller and larger quantities. The table below lists common SI prefixes.

SI Prefixes			
Prefix	**Abbreviation**	**Factor**	**Example**
kilo-	k	1,000	kilogram, 1 kg = 1,000 g
hecto-	h	100	hectoliter, 1 hL = 100 L
deka-	da	10	dekameter, 1 dam = 10 m
		1	meter, liter
deci-	d	0.1	decigram, 1 dg = 0.1 g
centi-	c	0.01	centimeter, 1 cm = 0.01 m
milli-	m	0.001	milliliter, 1 mL = 0.001 L
micro-	μ	0.000 001	micrometer, 1 μm = 0.000 001 m

SI Conversion Table		
SI units	**From SI to English**	**From English to SI**
Length		
kilometer (km) = 1,000 m	1 km = 0.621 mi	1 mi = 1.609 km
meter (m) = 100 cm	1 m = 3.281 ft	1 ft = 0.305 m
centimeter (cm) = 0.01 m	1 cm = 0.394 in.	1 in. = 2.540 cm
millimeter (mm) = 0.001 m	1 mm = 0.039 in.	
micrometer (μm) = 0.000 001 m		
nanometer (nm) = 0.000 000 001 m		
Area		
square kilometer (km^2) = 100 hectares	1 km^2 = 0.386 mi^2	1 mi^2 = 2.590 km^2
hectare (ha) = 10,000 m^2	1 ha = 2.471 acres	1 acre = 0.405 ha
square meter (m^2) = 10,000 cm^2	1 m^2 = 10.765 ft^2	1 ft^2 = 0.093 m^2
square centimeter (cm^2) = 100 mm^2	1 cm^2 = 0.155 in.^{2}	1 in.^{2} = 6.452 cm^2
Volume		
liter (L) = 1,000 mL = 1 dm^3	1 L = 1.057 fl qt	1 fl qt = 0.946 L
milliliter (mL) = 0.001 L = 1 cm^3	1 mL = 0.034 fl oz	1 fl oz = 29.575 mL
microliter (μL) = 0.000 001 L		
Mass		
kilogram (kg) = 1,000 g	1 kg = 2.205 lb	1 lb = 0.454 kg
gram (g) = 1,000 mg	1 g = 0.035 oz	1 oz = 28.349 g
milligram (mg) = 0.001 g		
microgram (μg) = 0.000 001 g		

Periodic Table of the Elements

APPENDIX

Each square on the table includes an element's name, chemical symbol, atomic number, and atomic mass.

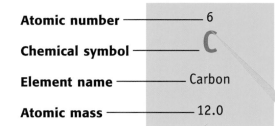

Atomic number —— 6
Chemical symbol —— C
Element name —— Carbon
Atomic mass —— 12.0

The background color indicates the type of element. Carbon is a nonmetal.

The color of the chemical symbol indicates the physical state at room temperature. Carbon is a solid.

Background
Metals
Metalloids
Nonmetals

Chemical Symbol
Solid
Liquid
Gas

Period 1

1
H
Hydrogen
1.0

	Group 1	Group 2		Group 3	Group 4	Group 5	Group 6	Group 7	Group 8	Group 9
Period 2	3 **Li** Lithium 6.9	4 **Be** Beryllium 9.0								
Period 3	11 **Na** Sodium 23.0	12 **Mg** Magnesium 24.3								
Period 4	19 **K** Potassium 39.1	20 **Ca** Calcium 40.1		21 **Sc** Scandium 45.0	22 **Ti** Titanium 47.9	23 **V** Vanadium 50.9	24 **Cr** Chromium 52.0	25 **Mn** Manganese 54.9	26 **Fe** Iron 55.8	27 **Co** Cobalt 58.9
Period 5	37 **Rb** Rubidium 85.5	38 **Sr** Strontium 87.6		39 **Y** Yttrium 88.9	40 **Zr** Zirconium 91.2	41 **Nb** Niobium 92.9	42 **Mo** Molybdenum 95.9	43 **Tc** Technetium (97.9)	44 **Ru** Ruthenium 101.1	45 **Rh** Rhodium 102.9
Period 6	55 **Cs** Cesium 132.9	56 **Ba** Barium 137.3		57 **La** Lanthanum 138.9	72 **Hf** Hafnium 178.5	73 **Ta** Tantalum 180.9	74 **W** Tungsten 183.8	75 **Re** Rhenium 186.2	76 **Os** Osmium 190.2	77 **Ir** Iridium 192.2
Period 7	87 **Fr** Francium (223.0)	88 **Ra** Radium (226.0)		89 **Ac** Actinium (227.0)	104 **Rf** Rutherfordium (261.1)	105 **Db** Dubnium (262.1)	106 **Sg** Seaborgium (263.1)	107 **Bh** Bohrium (262.1)	108 **Hs** Hassium (265)	109 **Mt** Meitnerium (266)

A row of elements is called a period.

A column of elements is called a group or family.

Lanthanides

58 **Ce** Cerium 140.1	59 **Pr** Praseodymium 140.9	60 **Nd** Neodymium 144.2	61 **Pm** Promethium (144.9)	62 **Sm** Samarium 150.4

Actinides

90 **Th** Thorium 232.0	91 **Pa** Protactinium 231.0	92 **U** Uranium 238.0	93 **Np** Neptunium (237.0)	94 **Pu** Plutonium 244.1

These elements are placed below the table to allow the table to be narrower.

Group 18

						2 **He** Helium 4.0

This zigzag line reminds you where the metals, nonmetals, and metalloids are.

Group 13	**Group 14**	**Group 15**	**Group 16**	**Group 17**	
5 **B** Boron 10.8	6 **C** Carbon 12.0	7 **N** Nitrogen 14.0	8 **O** Oxygen 16.0	9 **F** Fluorine 19.0	10 **Ne** Neon 20.2

			13 **Al** Aluminum 27.0	14 **Si** Silicon 28.1	15 **P** Phosphorus 31.0	16 **S** Sulfur 32.1	17 **Cl** Chlorine 35.5	18 **Ar** Argon 39.9

Group 10	**Group 11**	**Group 12**						
28 **Ni** Nickel 58.7	29 **Cu** Copper 63.5	30 **Zn** Zinc 65.4	31 **Ga** Gallium 69.7	32 **Ge** Germanium 72.6	33 **As** Arsenic 74.9	34 **Se** Selenium 79.0	35 **Br** Bromine 79.9	36 **Kr** Krypton 83.8
46 **Pd** Palladium 106.4	47 **Ag** Silver 107.9	48 **Cd** Cadmium 112.4	49 **In** Indium 114.8	50 **Sn** Tin 118.7	51 **Sb** Antimony 121.8	52 **Te** Tellurium 127.6	53 **I** Iodine 126.9	54 **Xe** Xenon 131.3
78 **Pt** Platinum 195.1	79 **Au** Gold 197.0	80 **Hg** Mercury 200.6	81 **Tl** Thallium 204.4	82 **Pb** Lead 207.2	83 **Bi** Bismuth 209.0	84 **Po** Polonium (209.0)	85 **At** Astatine (210.0)	86 **Rn** Radon (222.0)
110 **Uun*** Ununnilium (271)	111 **Uuu*** Unununium (272)	112 **Uub*** Ununbium (277)		114 **Uuq*** Ununquadium (285)		116 **Uuh*** Ununhexium (289)		118 **Uuo*** Ununoctium (293)

A number in parenthesis is the mass number of the most stable form of that element.

63 **Eu** Europium 152.0	64 **Gd** Gadolinium 157.3	65 **Tb** Terbium 158.9	66 **Dy** Dysprosium 162.5	67 **Ho** Holmium 164.9	68 **Er** Erbium 167.3	69 **Tm** Thulium 168.9	70 **Yb** Ytterbium 173.0	71 **Lu** Lutetium 175.0
95 **Am** Americium (243.1)	96 **Cm** Curium (247.1)	97 **Bk** Berkelium (247.1)	98 **Cf** Californium (251.1)	99 **Es** Einsteinium (252.1)	100 **Fm** Fermium (257.1)	101 **Md** Mendelevium (258.1)	102 **No** Nobelium (259.1)	103 **Lr** Lawrencium (262.1)

The official names and symbols for the elements greater than 109 will eventually be approved by a committee of scientists.

Math Refresher

Science requires an understanding of many math concepts. The following pages will help you review some important math skills.

Averages

An **average**, or **mean**, simplifies a list of numbers into a single number that *approximates* their value.

> **Example:** Find the average of the following set of numbers: 5, 4, 7, and 8.

Step 1: Find the sum.

$$5 + 4 + 7 + 8 = 24$$

Step 2: Divide the sum by the amount of numbers in your set. Because there are four numbers in this example, divide the sum by 4.

$$\frac{24}{4} = 6$$

The average, or mean, is **6.**

Ratios

A **ratio** is a comparison between numbers, and it is usually written as a fraction.

> **Example:** Find the ratio of thermometers to students if you have 36 thermometers and 48 students in your class.

Step 1: Make the ratio.

$$\frac{36 \text{ thermometers}}{48 \text{ students}}$$

Step 2: Reduce the fraction to its simplest form.

$$\frac{36}{48} = \frac{36 \div 12}{48 \div 12} = \frac{3}{4}$$

The ratio of thermometers to students is **3 to 4,** or $\frac{3}{4}$. The ratio may also be written in the form 3:4.

Proportions

A **proportion** is an equation that states that two ratios are equal.

$$\frac{3}{1} = \frac{12}{4}$$

To solve a proportion, first multiply across the equal sign. This is called cross-multiplication. If you know three of the quantities in a proportion, you can use cross-multiplication to find the fourth.

> **Example:** Imagine that you are making a scale model of the solar system for your science project. The diameter of Jupiter is 11.2 times the diameter of the Earth. If you are using a plastic-foam ball with a diameter of 2 cm to represent the Earth, what diameter does the ball representing Jupiter need to be?
>
> $$\frac{11.2}{1} = \frac{x}{2 \text{ cm}}$$

Step 1: Cross-multiply.

$$\frac{11.2}{1} \diagdown\!\!\!\!\diagup \frac{x}{2}$$

$$11.2 \times 2 = x \times 1$$

Step 2: Multiply.

$$22.4 = x \times 1$$

Step 3: Isolate the variable by dividing both sides by 1.

$$x = \frac{22.4}{1}$$

$$x = 22.4 \text{ cm}$$

You will need to use a ball with a diameter of **22.4 cm** to represent Jupiter.

Percentages

A **percentage** is a ratio of a given number to 100.

> **Example:** What is 85 percent of 40?

Step 1: Rewrite the percentage by moving the decimal point two places to the left.

$$.85$$

Step 2: Multiply the decimal by the number you are calculating the percentage of.

$$0.85 \times 40 = 34$$

85 percent of 40 is **34.**

Decimals

To **add** or **subtract decimals,** line up the digits vertically so that the decimal points line up. Then add or subtract the columns from right to left, carrying or borrowing numbers as necessary.

> **Example:** Add the following numbers: 3.1415 and 2.96.

Step 1: Line up the digits vertically so that the decimal points line up.

$$
\begin{array}{r}
3.1415 \\
+ \ 2.96 \\
\hline
\end{array}
$$

Step 2: Add the columns from right to left, carrying when necessary.

$$
\begin{array}{r}
1\ 1 \\
3.1415 \\
+ \ 2.96 \\
\hline
6.1015
\end{array}
$$

The sum is **6.1015.**

Fractions

Numbers tell you how many; **fractions** tell you *how much of a whole.*

> **Example:** Your class has 24 plants. Your teacher instructs you to put 5 in a shady spot. What fraction does this represent?

Step 1: Write a fraction with the total number of parts in the whole as the denominator.

$$\frac{?}{24}$$

Step 2: Write the number of parts of the whole being represented as the numerator.

$$\frac{5}{24}$$

$\frac{5}{24}$ of the plants will be in the shade.

Reducing Fractions

It is usually best to express a fraction in simplest form. This is called *reducing* a fraction.

> **Example:** Reduce the fraction $\frac{30}{45}$ to its simplest form.

Step 1: Find the largest whole number that will divide evenly into both the numerator and denominator. This number is called the greatest common factor (GCF).

factors of the numerator 30: 1, 2, 3, 5, 6, 10, **15,** 30

factors of the denominator 45: 1, 3, 5, 9, **15,** 45

Step 2: Divide both the numerator and the denominator by the GCF, which in this case is 15.

$$\frac{30}{45} = \frac{30 \div 15}{45 \div 15} = \frac{2}{3}$$

$\frac{30}{45}$ reduced to its simplest form is $\frac{2}{3}$.

Adding and Subtracting Fractions

To **add** or **subtract fractions** that have the **same denominator,** simply add or subtract the numerators.

> **Examples:**
> $$\frac{3}{5} + \frac{1}{5} = ? \quad \text{and} \quad \frac{3}{4} - \frac{1}{4} = ?$$

Step 1: Add or subtract the numerators.
$$\frac{3}{5} + \frac{1}{5} = \frac{4}{} \quad \text{and} \quad \frac{3}{4} - \frac{1}{4} = \frac{2}{}$$

Step 2: Write the sum or difference over the denominator.
$$\frac{3}{5} + \frac{1}{5} = \frac{4}{5} \quad \text{and} \quad \frac{3}{4} - \frac{1}{4} = \frac{2}{4}$$

Step 3: If necessary, reduce the fraction to its simplest form.
$$\frac{4}{5} \text{ cannot be reduced, and } \frac{2}{4} = \frac{1}{2}.$$

To **add** or **subtract fractions** that have **different denominators,** first find the least common denominator (LCD).

> **Examples:**
> $$\frac{1}{2} + \frac{1}{6} = ? \quad \text{and} \quad \frac{3}{4} - \frac{2}{3} = ?$$

Step 1: Write the equivalent fractions with a common denominator.
$$\frac{3}{6} + \frac{1}{6} = ? \quad \text{and} \quad \frac{9}{12} - \frac{8}{12} = ?$$

Step 2: Add or subtract.
$$\frac{3}{6} + \frac{1}{6} = \frac{4}{6} \quad \text{and} \quad \frac{9}{12} - \frac{8}{12} = \frac{1}{12}$$

Step 3: If necessary, reduce the fraction to its simplest form.
$$\frac{4}{6} = \frac{2}{3}, \text{ and } \frac{1}{12} \text{ cannot be reduced.}$$

Multiplying Fractions

To **multiply fractions,** multiply the numerators and the denominators together, and then reduce the fraction to its simplest form.

> **Example:**
> $$\frac{5}{9} \times \frac{7}{10} = ?$$

Step 1: Multiply the numerators and denominators.
$$\frac{5}{9} \times \frac{7}{10} = \frac{5 \times 7}{9 \times 10} = \frac{35}{90}$$

Step 2: Reduce.
$$\frac{35}{90} = \frac{35 \div 5}{90 \div 5} = \frac{7}{18}$$

Dividing Fractions

To **divide fractions,** first rewrite the divisor (the number you divide *by*) upside down. This is called the reciprocal of the divisor. Then you can multiply and reduce if necessary.

> **Example:**
> $$\frac{5}{8} \div \frac{3}{2} = ?$$

Step 1: Rewrite the divisor as its reciprocal.
$$\frac{3}{2} \rightarrow \frac{2}{3}$$

Step 2: Multiply.
$$\frac{5}{8} \times \frac{2}{3} = \frac{5 \times 2}{8 \times 3} = \frac{10}{24}$$

Step 3: Reduce.
$$\frac{10}{24} = \frac{10 \div 2}{24 \div 2} = \frac{5}{12}$$

Scientific Notation

Scientific notation is a short way of representing very large and very small numbers without writing all of the place-holding zeros.

> **Example:** Write 653,000,000 in scientific notation.

Step 1: Write the number without the place-holding zeros.

$$653$$

Step 2: Place the decimal point after the first digit.

$$6.53$$

Step 3: Find the exponent by counting the number of places that you moved the decimal point.

$$6.53000000$$

The decimal point was moved eight places to the left. Therefore, the exponent of 10 is positive 8. Remember, if the decimal point had moved to the right, the exponent would be negative.

Step 4: Write the number in scientific notation.

$$\mathbf{6.53 \times 10^8}$$

Area

Area is the number of square units needed to cover the surface of an object.

> **Formulas:**
> Area of a square = side × side
> Area of a rectangle = length × width
> Area of a triangle = $\frac{1}{2}$ × base × height
>
> **Examples:** Find the areas.

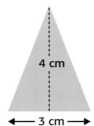

Triangle
Area = $\frac{1}{2}$ × base × height
Area = $\frac{1}{2}$ × 3 cm × 4 cm
Area = **6 cm²**

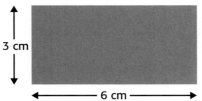

Rectangle
Area = length × width
Area = 6 cm × 3 cm
Area = **18 cm²**

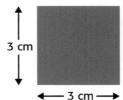

Square
Area = side × side
Area = 3 cm × 3 cm
Area = **9 cm²**

Volume

Volume is the amount of space something occupies.

> **Formulas:**
> Volume of a cube =
> side × side × side
>
> Volume of a prism =
> area of base × height
>
> **Examples:**
> Find the volume
> of the solids.

Cube
Volume = side × side × side
Volume = 4 cm × 4 cm × 4 cm
Volume = **64 cm³**

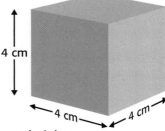

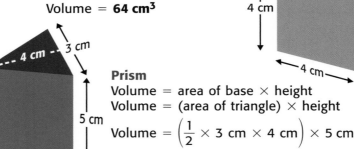

Prism
Volume = area of base × height
Volume = (area of triangle) × height
Volume = $\left(\frac{1}{2} \times 3 \text{ cm} \times 4 \text{ cm} \right)$ × 5 cm
Volume = 6 cm² × 5 cm
Volume = **30 cm³**

Glossary

A

alternating current (AC) electric current in which the charges continually switch from flowing in one direction to flowing in the reverse direction (16)

analog (AN uh LAHG) **signal** a signal whose properties, such as amplitude and frequency, can change continuously according to changes in the original information (75)

B

battery a device that is made of several cells and that produces an electric current by converting chemical energy into electrical energy (12)

binary (BIE neh ree) two; binary numbers contain only the digits 1 and 0 (76)

bit the name for each of the digits in a binary number (83)

byte a unit in which computers store and process information; equal to eight bits (83)

C

cathode-ray tube (CRT) a special vacuum tube in which a beam of electrons is projected onto a screen (79)

cell a device that produces an electric current by converting chemical energy into electrical energy (12)

central processing unit (CPU) the physical area in which a computer performs tasks (82)

circuit a complete, closed path through which electric charges flow (22)

circuit board a collection of hundreds of tiny circuits that supply electric current to the various parts of an electronic device (68)

computer an electronic device that performs tasks by processing and storing information (80)

conduction (electrical) a method of charging an object that occurs when electrons are transferred from one object to another by direct contact (7)

conductor (electrical) a material in which charges can move easily (9)

current a continuous flow of charge caused by the motion of electrons; the rate at which charge passes a given point; expressed in amperes (A) (15)

D

digital signal a series of electrical pulses that represents the digits of binary numbers (76)

diode (DIE OHD) an electronic component that allows electric current in only one direction (70)

direct current (DC) electric current in which the charges always flow in the same direction (16)

doping (DOHP eeng) the process of replacing a few atoms of a semiconductor with a few atoms of another substance that have a different number of valence electrons (69)

E

electric discharge the loss of static electricity as charges move off an object (10)

electric field the region around a charged particle that can exert a force on another charged particle (5)

electric force the force between charged objects (5)

electric motor a device that changes electrical energy into kinetic energy (50)

electric power the rate at which electrical energy is used to do work; expressed in watts (W) (19)

electrode the part of a cell through which charges enter or exit (12)

electrolyte in a cell, a mixture of chemicals that carries an electric current (12)

electromagnet a magnet that consists of a solenoid wrapped around an iron core (48)

electromagnetic induction the process by which an electric current is produced by a changing magnetic field (53)

electromagnetic wave a wave that can travel through space or matter and consists of changing electric and magnetic fields (78)

electromagnetism the interaction between electricity and magnetism (47)

G

generator a device that uses electromagnetic induction to convert kinetic energy into electrical energy (54)

H

hardware the parts or equipment that make up a computer (82)

I

induction a method of charging an object that occurs when charges in an uncharged object are rearranged without direct contact with a charged object (7)

input the information given to a computer (80)

input device a piece of hardware that feeds information to the computer (82)

insulator (electrical) a material in which charges cannot easily move (9)

integrated (IN tuh GRAYT ed) **circuit** an entire circuit containing many transistors and other electronic components formed on a single silicon chip (72)

Internet a huge computer network consisting of millions of computers that can all share information with one another (85)

L

law of electric charges the law that states that like charges repel and opposite charges attract (5)

load a device that uses electrical energy to do work (22)

M

magnet any material that attracts iron or materials containing iron (38)

magnetic field the region around a magnet in which magnetic forces can act (40)

magnetic force the force of repulsion or attraction between the poles of magnets (39)

memory the location where a computer stores information (80)

microprocessor an integrated circuit that contains many of a computer's capabilities on a single silicon chip (81)

modem a piece of computer hardware that allows computers to communicate over telephone lines (83)

O

Ohm's law the law that states the relationship between current (I), voltage (V), and resistance (R); expressed by the equation $I = \dfrac{V}{R}$ (19)

output the result of processing that is the final result or the proof of the task performed by a computer (80)

output device a piece of hardware on which a computer shows the results of performing a task (83)

P

parallel circuit a circuit in which different loads are on separate branches (25)

photocell the part of a solar panel that converts light into electrical energy (14)

poles the parts of a magnet where the magnetic effects are strongest (38)

potential difference energy per unit charge; specifically, the difference in energy per unit charge as a charge moves between two points in an electric circuit (same as voltage); expressed in volts (V) (13)

R

RAM (random-access memory) computer memory that stores information only while that information is being used (83)

resistance the opposition to the flow of electric charge; expressed in ohms (Ω) (17)

ROM (read-only memory) computer memory that cannot be added to or changed (83)

S

semiconductor (SEM i kuhn DUHK tor) a substance that conducts electric current better than an insulator but not as well as a conductor (69)

series circuit a circuit in which all parts are connected in a single loop (24)

signal something that represents information, such as a command, a sound, or a series of numbers and letters (74)

software a set of instructions or commands that tells a computer what to do; a computer program (84)

solenoid a coil of wire that produces a magnetic field when carrying an electric current (47)

static electricity the buildup of electric charges on an object (9)

T

telecommunication the sending of information across long distances by electronic means (74)

thermocouple a device that converts thermal energy into electrical energy (14)

transformer a device that increases or decreases the voltage of alternating current (56)

transistor an electronic component that can be used as an amplifier or a switch (71)

V

voltage the difference in energy per unit charge as a charge moves between two points in an electric circuit (same as potential difference); expressed in volts (V) (16)

W

watt (W) the unit used to express power (19)

Index

A **boldface** number refers to an illustration on that page.

A

alternating current (AC), 16, **16**
Ampère, André-Marie, 47
amperes, 15, 19
analog signals, 74–76, **75, 76, 78**
armature, 50, **50**
atoms
    electric charge and, 4–5
auroras, 45, **45**
automobiles. *See* cars
averages, 108

B

batteries, 12, **12,** 13, **13,** 16–17
binary numbers, 76
birds, 44
bits, 83
breaker boxes, 26–27
bytes, 83

C

cars
    batteries, **13**
    painting, 5
cathode-ray tubes (CRT), 79
CD players, **76,** 76–77, **77**
CDs (compact discs), **76,** 76–77
cells, electric, **12,** 12–13
central processing unit (CPU), 82, **82**
charge. *See* electric charge
circuit boards, 68, **68**
circuit breakers, 26–27, **27**
circuits, 22–27. *See also* electric circuits
    integrated, 72, **72**
communication technology
    analog signals, 74–76, **75, 76, 78**
    CDs (compact discs), 76, **76**
    digital signals, **76,** 76–77, **77**
    radio, 78, **78**
    records, 76, **76**
    telegraph, 74, **74**
    telephone, 75, **75**
    television, 79, **79**

commutator, 50, **50**
compasses, 43, 44, **44, 46,** 47
computers, 80–85
    basic functions, 80, **80**
    defined, 80
    hardware, **82,** 82–83, **83**
    history, 81
    Internet, 85, **85**
    software, 84, **84**
concept mapping
    defined, 104
conduction
    of charge, 7, **7,** 17
conductors, 9
conservation
    of charge, 7, 30
conversion tables
    SI, 105
CPU (central processing unit), 82, **82**
CRT (cathode-ray tube), 79
current, 15. *See also* amperes; electric current

D

decimals, 109
digital signals, **76,** 76–77, **77**
diodes, 70, **70**
direct current (DC), 16, **16,** 70
domains, 40–42, **41**
doorbells, 49, **49**
doping, 69
dry cells, 13

E

ears, 90
Earth
    core, 44
    magnetic field, 43, **43,** 44–45
earthquakes, 75
electrical energy
    alternative sources of, 14
    atoms and, 4–5
    electric charge and, 4–11, 30
    generating, 55, 57, **57**
    measurement of, 20–21, 31
    resistance and, 17–19, 31
electrical storms, **10,** 10–11, 30
electric cells, **12,** 12–13
electric charge, 5–9
    conduction, 7
    conservation of, 7
    detecting, 8

friction and, 6, **6**
    induction, 7
    law of, 5, **5**
    static electricity and, 9, **9**
electric circuits, 22–27
    defined, 22
    failures, **26,** 26–27, **27,** 31
    household, 26–27
    parts of, **22,** 22–23, **23,** 31
    types of, 23–25, **24, 25,** 30
electric current, 12–13, 15–21, 31
    alternating, 16, **16,** 55–56, 70
    diodes and, **70**
    direct, 16, **16,** 70
    magnetic force and, 49, **49, 51, 52,** 52–54, **53, 54**
    transistors, **71,** 71–72, **72**
electric discharge, 10
electric eels, **17**
electric fields, 5, 15
electric force, 5, 30
electric generators, **54,** 54–55, **55**
electricity. *See also* electrical energy; electric current
    from magnetism, 52–57
electric motors, 50, **50**
electric power, 19–20, 31. *See also* electrical energy
electrodes, 12, **12**
electrolytes, 12
electromagnetic induction, 53, **53,** 54, **54**
    applications, **54,** 54–57, **55, 56, 57**
electromagnetism, 65. *See also* magnets
    applications, 49–51
    discovery of, **46,** 46–47
    electric current and, 49, **49,** 50, **50,** 51, **51, 52,** 52–54, **53, 54**
    uses of, 47–51
electromagnets, 42, 48
electronic components, 68–73
    circuit boards, 68, **68**
    diodes, 70, **70**
    integrated circuits, 72, **72,** 86
    semiconductors and, 69, **69**
    transistors, **71,** 71–72, **72,** 86
    vacuum tubes, 73, **73**
electrons
    electrical energy and, **4,** 15, **15**
    in electric cells, **12**
    electric charge, 5–9, **7, 8**
    magnetic fields and, 40
electroscopes, 8, **8**
elements. *See* periodic table
ENIAC (Electronic Numerical Integrator and Computer), 81, **81**

INDEX

Credits

Abbreviations used: (t) top, (c) center, (b) bottom, (l) left, (r) right, (bkgd) background

ILLUSTRATIONS

All illustrations, unless noted below, by Holt, Rinehart and Winston.

Table of Contents v, Stephen Durke/Washington Artists; vi, Dan Geehan/Koralik Associates

Chapter One Page 4(t), Blake Thornton/Rita Marie; 4(b), Stephen Durke/Washington Artists; 5, John White/The Neis Group; 7(l), Stephen Durke/Washington Artists; 10, Dan Stuckenschneider/Uhl Studios Inc.; 12, 14, Mark Heine; 15, 16, Geoff Smith/Scott Hull; 18, Will Nelson/Sweet Reps; 21(cr), Boston Graphics; 26, Dan McGeehan/Koralik Associates.

Chapter Two Page 40, 41, 42, Stephen Durke/Washington Artists; 43, Mark Persyn; 44(b), Stephen Durke/Washington Artists; 46, 47, 49, Sidney Jablonski; 50, Patrick Gnan/Deborah Wolfe Ltd.; 51, Stephen Durke/ Washington Artists; 52, Mark Heine; 53, 54(t), Mark Persyn; 54(b), 55(t), David Fischer; 55(b), John Francis, 56, Tony Randazzo; 57, Dan Stuckenschneider/Uhl Studios Inc.; 60(l), Sidney Jablonski; 60(r), Mark Persyn; 61, David Fischer; 63, Stephen Durke/Washington Artists.

Chapter Three Page 69, 70(c), Stephen Durke/Washington Artists; 70(b), Gary Ferster; 71, Blake Thornton/Rita Marie; 72, Gary Ferster; 75, 76(tl), Dan Stuckenschneider/Uhl Studios Inc.; 76(b), 77(tr), Stephen Durke/Washington Artists; 78, Blake Thornton/Rita Marie; 79, Dan Stuckenschneider/Uhl Studios Inc.; 80, Preface, Inc.; 85, Blake Thornton/Rita Marie; 86(bl), Stephen Durke/Washington Artists; 86(br), Blake Thornton/Rita Marie; 88(cl), 89(tr), Gary Ferster.

LabBook Page 97(tr), Gary Ferster; 97(br), Dave Joly.

Appendix Page 106, 107, Kristy Sprott.

PHOTOGRAPHY

Cover and Title Page: IT Stock International/Index Stock Imagery/ Picture Quest

Table of Contents v(t), Richard Megna/Fundamental Photographs; v(b), Peter Van Steen/HRW Photo; vi(c), Paul Silverman/Fundamental Photographs; vi(b), vii(t), Sam Dudgeon/HRW Photo; vii(b), Pekka Parviainen/ Photo Researchers, Inc.

Feature Borders: Unless otherwise noted below, all images ©2001 PhotoDisc/HRW: "Health Watch" 65, 90, dumbbell, Sam Dudgeon/HRW Photo, aloe vera and EKG, Victoria Smith/HRW Photo, basketball, ©1997 Radlund & Associates for Artville, shoes and Bubbles, Greg Geisler; "Science, Technology, and Society" robot 34,Greg Geisler; "Science Fiction" 91, saucers, Ian Christopher/Greg Geisler, book, HRW, bkgd, Stock Illustration Source; "Across the Sciences" 35, 64, all images by HRW.

Chapter One: Page 2-3 Peter Van Steen/HRW Photo; 3 HRW Photo; 6(l,r), Victoria Smith/HRW Photo; 8(b), Stephanie Morris/HRW Photo; 9(b), Peter Van Steen/HRW Photo; 11, Jack "Thunderhead" Corso; 17(t), Patricia Ceisel/ Visuals Unlimited; 17(b), David R. Frazier Photolibrary; 18, Takeshi Takahara/ Photo Researchers, Inc.; 19, Science Photo Library/Photo Researchers, Inc.; 20(br), Richard Hanes/HRW Photo; 21, Visuals Unlimited; 22(l), Richard T. Nowitz/Photo Researchers, Inc.; 27(t), Paul Silverman/Fundamental Photographs; 29 Victoria Smith/HRW Photo; 32(t), Victoria Smith/HRW Photo; 34(t), Corbis-Bettmann; 34(b), Bill Ross/ Corbis; 35(l), Daniel Osborne, University of Alaska/Detlev Ban Ravenswaay/Science Photo Library/Photo Researchers, Inc.; 35(r), STARLab, Stanford University.

Chapter Two: Page 36-37 Bill Ross/CORBIS; 37 HRW Photo; 39(bl,bc,br), 40, Richard Megna/ Fundamental Photographs; 45(l), Pekka Parviainen/Photo Researchers Inc; 47, SuperStock; 48, Tom Tracy/The Stock Shop; 64, The Image Bank; 65, Howard Sochurek.

Chapter Three: Page 66-67 Telegraph Colour Library/FPG International; 67 HRW Photo; 74, Dr. E.R. Degginger/Color-Pic, Inc.; 75, Yoav Levy/PhotoTake; 79 (inset), Corbis Images; 81(l), Corbis/Bettmann; 81(r), SuperStock; 84, monitor, HRW Photo; 84, web site, HRW Photo; 87, SuperStock; 90, Peter Van Steen/HRW Photo.

LabBook "LabBook Header": "L," Corbis Images, "a," Letraset Phototone, "b" and "B," HRW, "o" and "k," Images ©2001 PhotoDisc/HRW; 93(c), Michelle Bridwell/HRW Photo; 93(br), Image © 2001 PhotoDisc, Inc.; 94(cl), Victoria Smith/HRW Photo; 94(bl), Stephanie Morris/HRW Photo; 95(tr), Jana Birchum/HRW Photo; 95(b), Peter Van Steen/HRW Photo; 99, David Young-Wolf/PhotoEdit.

Sam Dudgeon/HRW Photo Page viii-1, 13(b); 14; 20(t,bl,bc); 22(b,c); 27(b); 31; 33(b); 38; 39(t); 41; 42; 44; 58; 59; 62-63; 68; 70-73; 76; 80-81; 82; 83; 86; 88; 92; 93(b); 94(br,t); 95(tl); 96; 98; 100; 101-103.

John Langford/HRW Photo Page 7; 8(tl,tr); 9(t); 13(t); 20(cl); 22(r); 23; 24; 25; 26; 30; 32(b); 33(t); 93(t).

lf-Check Answers

Chapter 1—Introduction to Electricity

Page 7: Plastic wrap is charged by friction as it is pulled off the roll.

Page 20: $E = P \times t$; $E = 200\text{ W} \times 2\text{ h} = 400\text{ Wh}$

Students will have to use data from the table on page 20 to answer this question.

Page 23: Yes; a microwave oven is an example of a load because it uses electrical energy to do work.

Chapter 2—Electromagnetism

Page 48: No; an electromagnet is produced when the magnetic field of the coil of wire causes the domains in the core to line up. Wood does not contain domains and therefore cannot be the core of an electromagnet.

Chapter 3—Electronic Technology

No self-check question for this chapter.